MAGICK

Magick at WinterFest this year.
Harpist Yasmine Russell used her 36 String Electric Harp to create an Orchestra of Harps at Winterfest 2019

SPELLING IT OUT - THE EDITORS RAVE
KNOW THY SELF

This issue is about things that you thought you knew and perhaps didn't. It started off about something completely different (The Elements) and then it evolved into what you have in your hands. That's how you know when magick is happening. It is not always a working of your will. Sometimes you will something, but it becomes something else better. Like the young (and not so young) women (and men) who come to me wanting love spells. "I want this person to fall in love with me." I talk them out of it most of the time and persuade them to do love spells for love instead. And they thank me for it. Some times focusing on just one thing does not allow the magickal process of change to happen. We all know how it feels to not want to lose a pet but spending thousands of $$$ to keep the pet here when it really wants to leave for its next incarnation, not only prolongs the suffering of the animal but it also prevents you seeing where that energy will come back into your life and in what form. There is great magick in not forcing your will, in surrendering to the cycles of change and seeing in what form, the will of the universe, will grant you what you wish for.

There is also great wisdom in not believing everything that you see in the media, social or otherwise. Sometimes if you hear something that gives you an emotional reaction it is way to easy to react rather than research. There is GREAT POWER in KNOWING 'IT' FOR THYSELF. It's all about the punctuation really. "Know Thyself" can mean many things depending on the inflection you use when you say it. Try it, Don't just take my word for it!

It saddens me deeply that young people are taking their lives in an emotional reaction, because the media has filled them with a fear of their future. No one can know the full truth of any much debated subject unless they have 1st hand experience. People who tell you things often do so for their own agendas. A person who speaks with pseudo-authority can trick anyone who does not have personal experience of the matters discussed. Are the scientists who are pro-climate change, and on the payroll of the governments who see this as a wonderful way to get the public behind new taxes, any better than the scientist that work for the drug companies that tout the latest chemical wonder without knowing its full side effects, to fill the coffers of big business. Still, some drugs are useful but many are dangerous. If natural therapies were as dangerous as commercial drugs they would have been banned years ago. Still I would not swallow anything that any other recommends, natural or allopathic, without doing a lot of research myself.

Change is constant and necessary in magick. Scientists are right, our climate is changing. However, if you speak to our old wise ones we can see that the climate has always changed. There are larger cycles. The Indigenous Australians will tell you of the great cycles of drought and flooding rains that have been the norm in Australia for 20,000 years. The Mayan calendar tells us that too. Australian weather witch, Indigo Jones, predicted this current cycle from examining solar flares and spots. Carbon is not the issue. All the magicians who look up to our sky can see the moon being mined & the ionosphere being bombarded with space junk and by microwaves. All of our weather comes from the stream of electrons and other particles from the sun hitting our ionosphere. Our greed for social media and connectivity is doing far more damage than carbon. Carbon gets breathed in by our plants, and breathed out of our volcanos.

Anyway I'm not trying to tell you anything, I am just trying to get you to think and do some research for yourself and then you will Know for Thyself.

Every Blessing to you - Shé

Magick Magazine No. 9

TABLE OF CONTENTS

Our theme this issue is THINGS MOST PEOPLE DONT KNOW ABOUT MAGICK. .
So find out what The Magick Magazine uncovered to share with you!

SPELLING IT OUT - THE EDITORS RAVE	2	THE LANDMARK HAUNTED BOOKSHOP IN MELBOURNE	48
TABLE OF CONTENTS	3	FALLS VICTIM TO RELIGIOUS VILIFICATION	
THE MAGICK OF FAERIES, TREE & NATURE SPIRITS	5	THE MAGIC OF TOUCH	50
ANCIENT MAGICK IN MODERN ANIME SUBCULTURE	6	THE WEEKLY SEER	55
WENDY RULE : BEFORE & AFTER LIFE	8	AN ANCIENT STORY RETOLD THROUGH MUSIC	56
THE RENDEZVOUS TEA ROOM REOPENS	9	THE END OF AN ERA	58
GOOD OMENS:REVIEW	10	LEAVE BEHIND YOUR PAST	59
TALISMAN SPELLS	12	LIVING VIKING TRADITIONS	60
WINTERFEST	14	NEPTUNES SCEPTER	62
FIONA HORNE ROCKS ON	16	WITCH'S ALMANAC	64
THE PATHWAY TO THE GODDESS	18	HELP PAGANISM TO BECOME A RECOGNISED DENOMINATION	71
THE FERTILE MOON	26	THEDA BARA	72
VIKING WEDDING	28	BOOKS BY SHÉ D'MONTFORD	73
BELTANE FIRE	30	A WILD DOLPHIN QUEST	74
SPIRIT FESTIVAL 2019	31	READERS FUNNY PHOTOS	76
HERMETIC INVOCATION TO HELIOS - GOD OF BRILLIANCE	32	MAGICKAL ADS	77
THE DE LAURENCE MAGICKAL REVOLUTION	34	MAGICKAL COURSE	78
DID ALEISTER CROWLEY FAKE HIS OWN DEATH ?? TWICE ??	44		

M A G I C K 9 I S B N 9 7 8 - 0 - 9 9 4 3 5 4 1 - 5 - 0

Disclaimer: By law, we need to add this statement. This book is for educational purposes only and does not claim to prevent or cure any disease. The advice and methods in this book should not be construed as financial, medical or psychological treatment. Please seek advice from a professional if you have serious financial, medical or psychological issues. By purchasing and reading this book, you understand that results are not guaranteed. In light of this, you understand that in the event that this book does not work or causes harm in any area of your life, you agree that you do not hold Shé D'Montford, Shambhallah Awareness Centre, Happy Medium Publishing, its employees or affiliates liable for any damages you may experience or incur. The primary reason for this publication is entertainment and education about Pagan practices. While Shambhallah Awareness Centre has used all reasonable endeavours to ensure the information in this book is as accurate as possible, it gives no warranty or guarantee that the material, information, or publications made accessible by them are not fit for any use whatsoever nor does that excuse you from using your common sense. Shambhallah Awareness Centre and Rev. Dr S. D'Montford accepts no liability or responsibility for any loss or damage whatsoever suffered as a result of direct or indirect use or application of any material, publication or information obtained from them. These images qualifies as fair use under copyright law as use rationale, used for critical commentary and discussion by a non-profit organisation. Any other uses of this image may be copyright infringement.

Our Cover Photo Credits & Inside Cover
Personal Information
Mara aka Psychara Forest witch & artist in France. Owner of Psypuffs + art page Psychara art
Also at instagram @psychara !
Model, make-up: Psychara
Photographer, retoucher: Alexändra Sleäze Photography
Become a Patron: https://www.patreon.com/AlexandraSleaze

This magazine brought to you by Happy Medium Publishing a division of Shambhallah Awareness Center. This extract is based on information supplied by the Registrar of the Australian Business Register. Tax Concession status: THE SHAMBHALLAH CHURCH INC, a Charitable Fund, is endorsed to access the following tax concessions: Tax concession From GST Concession 01 Jul 2005., Income Tax Exemption 01 Jul 2000. Deductible Gift Recipient: THE SHAMBHALLAH CHURCH INC operates the following Funds, Authorities or Institutions. Gifts to these Funds, Authorities or Institutions may be deductible from 01 Jul 2000

Magick spelled with a "K," in the old Scottish fashion, indicates a number of belief systems that teach how to make changes in the external world according to your will. The "k" makes a distinction between deeply held beliefs & mere stage prestidigitation or trickery, as is indicated when spelled as "magic."

Proudly Australian owned, operated & produced. A not-for-profit publication. Contributed articles are not the personal opinions of this magazine or editors. Some content royalty free. Some content qualifies as fair use under copyright law as use rationale, this being some images & credited quotes, used for critical commentary & discussion of the topics by an educational non-profit organisation. Any other uses of this content may be copyright infringement. All other content © held by Shambhallah Awareness Centre, The Happy Medium Publishing Company & Shé D'Montford 2019 - However views expressed do not represent those of the publisher or associates.

THE HAPPY MEDIUM PUBLISHING COMPANY
THE MESSAGE IS IN THE MEDIUM

A Fairy in the Tree in Sarah Fay's Yard.
Photograph by Fay Gregory

THE MAGICK OF FAERIES, TREE & NATURE SPIRITS

Nature is so healing and beautiful, but do you really know how magickal nature really is? Have you heard the whispers in the trees? The hypnotic music drifting on the breeze? The faces on the trunks of trees that seem so wise and you get the feeling that they just seem to know more than we do? These are the faeries, tree spirits and nature spirits that live in secret in trees, flowers, wild gardens and bushland and forests etc They look after nature and protect her as best as they can, which would not be easy in these times of money and greed.

And this brings me to why we do not see these amazing creatures, as we are not their favourite inhabitant on this beautiful mother earth. We destroy so much of nature that they have become untrusting of us, and you have to win this trust back. So for the many nature loving witches, such as myself , we have a much better chance of coming across these elemental beings than most people. But we still need to work at it. They also can mainly be seen as energy only, so little lights or orbs, or you may just sense their presence . As a lot of the time they are in different realms to us and may cross in and out of our realm so quickly.

Here are some of the main groups of these magickal little creatures and a bit about them.

The Faeries are little elemental energies that are like natures angels. They help the tree spirits and other nature spirits to protect nature . They live in another realm that co-exists with our world, a Faery Realm it is sometimes known as. They are also known as the little people and there are legends that go back as long as we have inhabited this earth about the Faeries. Some are mischievous and naughty , and some are gentle, fun and helpful. They can often aid humans work , especially witches , pagans and nature lovers. To connect with Faeries be kind to nature, hang sprigs of thyme in your house or grow it in your garden. Wait until the veil between realms is thinner, at Beltane and Samhain. You can leave out little offerings of milk and honey, and send out the message you want to connect with them, then be patient. Also protect your self whenever doing any of these rituals. There are many types of faeries, have fun connecting with these special beings.

Tree Spirit's also called Dryads, originate in the Celtic countries. They live in trees and protect them. They are playful and are usually referred to as female. If you see them they are also wisps of energy or light and are sometimes lightly coloured. They are more open to communicating with humans than faeries and I did talk about connecting with them in my story about connecting with trees in one of the previous Magick magazines. They particularly love willows , and this is where I seem to get the most response when I connect with tree spirits , with the beautiful Moon Goddess Willow on my place. The Dryads gave the secret of tree magick to the Druids , and they also make beautiful music that you may hear on the breeze. To connect with them, pick a tree and connect with it as in the previous Magick Magazine.

Some say Nature Spirit's are beautiful deities who work with the faeries etc to keep the forests full of trees, to help the plants grow and also to protect nature. They are said to be divine beings that control natural phenomena and are said to help create all of nature from the beginning. They are sometimes thought to include Gods and Goddesses such as Mother Nature or Pan.

To me nature spirits really include all the magickal beings that work to protect nature , I do not feel that they are any particular type, and can include the above Faeries and Tree Spirit's as well as Deva's ,Sylphs, Nymphs , Deities etc they are also the small beings who inhabit many crystals. They are also approached in the same manner , with respect to nature and Mother Earth. And to connect with them is to connect with nature.

Hope this has helped you to learn more about the magick that is all around us and explore the realms of the Nature Spirits.

Magick and Blessings

Sarah- Fay

ANCIENT MAGICK in MODERN ANIME SUBCULTURE

Witches and magick disguised as fantasy is fast becoming a pop culture, seeping into tv and Netflix; enticing children and entertaining geeks and cosplayers alike. Anime, since high school days and mornings late for the bus watching Sailor Moon; with its occultish allegories that have had subtly branched an Asian-esque influence to my magick. From the beautiful moralistic magick of Studio Ghibli, Japanese mythological creatures that make Pokemons, Aegyptian mythos that creates Yu-Gi-Oh cards and the spirit entrapments of Yokai Watch among a few. Thank the gods for Netflix, subtitles and chill.

Honouring falial remembrance of the dead is an important element of ancestor Shinto worship. Tales told about the ghosts of deceased family members and other spirits are woven into stories not only to both entertain and amuse, but also serve as warnings (a preferred mode for elders ensuring good behaviour in unruly children). If deceased family members were not honoured and respected, their spirits would wreck havoc on whomever had forgotten them. The type of person when alive and also mode of death of the deceased can affect spirits motives. Evil spirits can be bound to do good by the proper spells and rituals.

Shinto believe two worlds exist which often collide, the human world and the dwelling place of ancestors, demons, and gods. Unusual markings and peculiar features found in natural places of beauty are sacred, physical manifestations of gods, or the spirit of the place, Kami. Oni is the name for evil spirits and demons, usually invisible and felt by foreboding dread, temporary powers only if evoked. Obake are ghosts that require certain rituals to be sent away or bind from real harm. Obake like to cause mischief to the living, and mortal harm. Spirits of dead animals can even possess humans, trickster fox the most well known. Almost anything can possess a human, and when they do, they are all known as Tsukimono, the Possessing Things. Takup appear in dreams and pass on messages from the otherside, or perhaps lead an individual on a spiritual quest; heeding if the sleeper awakes before physically returning to their body, else they shall die.

- (Yo)-mysterious, bewitching, unearthly. An attraction to something beyond the normal. Etherally beautiful and charming.
- (Kai)-mystery, wonder, strange. Kai enacts a sense of horror, or the fear of the unknown.
- Yokai is the name for the folkloric creatures of Japan and mysterious events such as strange weather, mysterious illnesses, strange phenomenons, monsters, evil spirits of rivers and mountains, demons, goblins, apparitions, shape-shifters, ghosts, mysterious occurrences, and magic.

Anything that can not be understood or explained, are Yokai and classified into four seperate categories:
- Kaiju (Kai; mysterious) - (Ju; beast), meaning monster.
- Choshizen (Cho; super) - (Shizen; natural), meaning the supernatural, including mysterious phenomenons.
- Henge (Hen; strange) - (Ge; change, transform), meaning shape-shifters like foxes and cats.
- Yurei (Yu; dim) - (Rei; spirit), meaning ghosts, and the spirits of the dead.

A distinct woven thread ensures their mystery today, ancestors and long-ago gods are kept alive and a reverence for nature, absorbed into mainstream western popular culture. If you are serious about your magick and anime, or knowledgeable of history and shinto; cosplay can be enchanted with glamour magick.

Transcripts from thousands of years past, show Yokai were real and both revered and feared. 1st century text 'Junshiden', reads "the Yokai was in the Imperial Court for a very long time" instilling a sense of unnatural anxiety and foreboding. 772CE, in the 'Shoku Nihongi', a ritual cleansing was recommended to "clear away the Yokai". The bestiary 'Yokai Chakutocho classifies Yokai for the first time. Nihon Shoki (The Chronicle of Japan), tells of the 'Age of the Gods'; creation mythos, and a time when gods ruled earth before leaving humanity to rule itself. The Engishiki, a collected work of fifty books of compiling laws, practices, rituals and prayers of Shinto. The Fudoki, categorises spirit inhabitants of nature and their associated legends, the Kami.

Bio: Belinda Annesley; Priestess, Author and Psychic Creatrix.

www.witchesandbritchers.blogspot.com

Image: Credit: "Animie Girl in A Magickal Forest" Royalty Free Wallpaper

WENDY RULE : BEFORE & AFTER LIFE

See, I've come to the centre now
Here I usher the souls that pass
Over the threshold go
Over the threshold go
There to become the seed
Bidding the flower to grow
All life into the dark goes
Into the womb, the tomb
Into the hunger
Into the teeth falls
Into the mouth crawls
Into the cavern called
Into the centre
Life feeds, swallows its own tail
Filling its belly full,
Full of its children
All life into the dark goes
Into the womb, the tomb
Into the hunger
Birth am I
And Death am I

And woman am I
I am before and after Life
Deep in the Earth
A death and a birth
A quickening flame
That whispered my name
I honoured the call
Taking the throne
I wasn't alone
A spark of desire
Had kindled my fire
And freed me
Birth am I
And Death am I
And woman am I
I am before and after Life
Something below
I wanted to know Eager to feed
I swallowed the seed
And now that I'm fed I am alive, alive
With all this glorious red!

From Wendy's new album: Persephone

Earth Spirit-Natures Clothing & Giftware
Rear 200 Anson St - Orange - NSW - 2800
Ph. 02 6362 9773
http://earthspiritnatures.com.au
https://www.facebook.com/earthspiritshop

THE RENDEZVOUS TEA ROOM REOPENS

It quickly became 'Standing Room Only' as Kate Denning reopened the Rendezvous Tea Room on Friday 19th July at 5.30pm. Surprisingly beautiful music in a jazz/blues/classical fusion was provided by Rob Reeves, Amanda Wallace and Lucy Francis (on cello) of "Harmonic Avenue" & "Bloodwood." Kate describes her inspiration to reopen the tea room after Luke Qudrelli's untimely death in the infamous Lime Scooter accident in Brisbane, this way: "I drove past the tea room only the other day and dropped in just to pay my respects to Luke and saw the 'For Lease' sign and next thing I know is that I'm ringing up the owner of the building. So here we are, I am re-opening The Rendezvous Tea Room to honour Luke's Memory. To continue what he has created. A loving warm space for people to come. A place to help you find your purpose. A safe place to talk to someone. A place to learn and be supported. Maybe you have a class or workshop and need somewhere to hold it. Maybe you have spiritual products you have created and looking for somewhere to promote them. Come and meet some of the amazing psychic people that are working here"

You can give Kate a call now on 0411 254 880 to book your personal tea leaf reading or to organise a fun themed psychic tea party for your friends.

GOOD OMENS: REVIEW

Good Omens: Neil Gaiman says 'global idiocy' of 2019 perfect for Armageddon drama

Apocalyptic comedy drama starring Michael Sheen & David Tennant debuted on Amazon Prime Video

The apocalypse is coming and humanity is doomed, unless we learn to look at life through the innocence and simplicity (or not so simply, if you are the anti-christ) of our childhood. This is the message of "Good Omens." 2019 is the perfect backdrop for Good Omens, the all-star, fantasy novel, 6-hour adaptation, which is one of the most hotly-anticipated streaming/TV shows of the year, says writer Neil Gaiman. The comedy drama, which features Michael Sheen and David Tennant as an angel and a demon teaming up to try and sabotage the end of the world, is based on the 1990 best-seller penned by the literary dream team of Gaiman and the late Terry Pratchett. A big-budget collaboration between Amazon Prime Video and the BBC, Good Omens has attracted an A-list cast including Jon Hamm, Miranda Richardson, Derek Jacobi and Jack Whitehall. The story, which begins with the armies of Good and Evil amassing and the Four Horsemen of the Apocalypse ready to ride, makes much more sense in the age of Trump and Brexit, believes Gaiman.

'Global idiocy'

"When the book was written, the only worry Terry and I had was that we were in this sudden new-found Glasnost-y magickal world of 1990, when history was over and everything seemed at peace," the 'Sandman' and 'Doctor Who' writer, Gaiman added: "The idea of Armageddon seemed further away than ever. Right now the nuclear clock is ticking, closer and closer to midnight. Now international terrorism is at an all-time high and so is polarisation. Global idiocy is at an all time high, which makes it incredibly appropriate – we're suddenly timely." Director Douglas Mackinnon, who won an Emmy for his work on the BBC's 'Sherlock,' said: "The only thing the book didn't predict was the Internet. We've touched it up for the present day and it's very much set in 2019." The six-part series debuted on Amazon Prime and then runs later in the year on BBC2. So, you can have the binge-watch option or the delayed gratification in the serialised style. "We can have our cake and eat it on this one, because Amazon Prime are going to drop it all and people will binge watch and they're going to drop it six months later on the BBC which will show it weekly and people can get it weekly," said Gaiman. "And at that point we can find out which people enjoyed more."

Sheen stars as angel and rare book dealer Aziraphale, with Tennant playing his opposite number, the fast living demon Crowley, both of whom have lived amongst Earth's mortals since The Beginning and have grown rather too fond of the lifestyle and of each other.

THE END HAS BEGUN. GOOD OMENS: NOW SHOWING ON PRIME

Talisman Spells

This is a talisman engraved with the hermetic and cabalistic formulas used by Catherine de Medici, one of the most successful queens of the Elizabethan period. It was made for her by her court astrologer, Cosimo Ruggeri, son of the astrologer of the Medici (Pope's) family in Florence.

Catherine's cultural background in fact was part of the Neoplatonic, Hermetic and Astrological Tradition that had already firmly rooted to the Valois court. Strongly influenced by Marsilio Ficino, she was interested in the science of the stars as "an aspiration both of Florentine Platonism and of the french philosophical and prophetic tradition.." says Luisa Capodieci, art historian, in her book "Medicaea Medaea. Art, Astres et Pouvoir à la Cour de Cathérine de Médicis".

Catherine's talisman was made from metals melted during favorable astrological signs and then mixed with human and goat blood. The actual talisman, which the Queen utilised, was destroyed when she died, but a copy can be found at the Bibliotheque Nationale de France in Paris.

Many believe it was created to attract love. Catherine had many lovers but this was a talisman of power. One side has depicted Jupiter, seated on a eagle, and a Erashigal, the Babylonian power broking goddess depicted with beak and bird claws. On the revers Venus, goddess of beauty and love, accompanied by the engraved names of Goetia genii of power, including Asmodeus.

Let's look closer to the images and words engraved on the talisman. The female figure with the bird head and eagle feet is holding a dart with her right hand and with her left hand an object like a convex mirror or a lens. The female figure on the other side is holding a heart in her right hand and a comb in her left hand. We can recognise in those two pictures two magical images of

Agrippa in his "Three Books of Occult Philosophy" says: *"From the operations of Venus they made an Image, which was available for favour, and benevolence, at the very hour it ascending into Pisces, the form of which was the Image of a woman having the head of a bird, and feet of an Eagle, holding a dart in her hand."*

The image of Jupiter according to the Picatrix should be engraved on a talisman...: *"If you wish to be esteemed by officials and judges, make under the influence of Jupiter the form of a handsome man with ample robes riding an eagle in crystal stone in the hour of Jupiter when Jupiter is in the ascendant and his exaltation. It is true that officials and judges will esteem those that carry these images with them."*

We can also see on the talisman among other obscure names and glyphs:

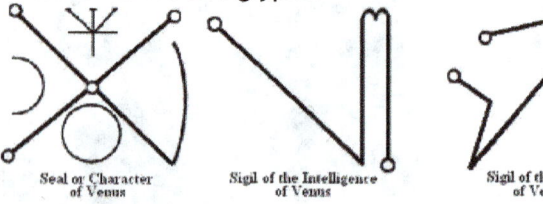

- The seal of Venus
- The sigil of Hagiel, the Intelligence of Venus and his name
- The name of the Angel of Venus, as Anael and as Haniel
- The name of the Goetia genii Asmodeus as Asmodel

Words engraved on the talisman are various names of Goetic beings of power:

- Gersiver
- Dray De Min
- Frenetic
- Draganiel
- Talian
- Penel
- Ai
- Ipos
- Filiac
- Disdras
- Nechar
- Opribal

If this was solely Catherine's love talisman then it didn't work too well, as her husband, Henri II kept favouring his famed mistress, Diane de Poitiers till his death. However, as a talisman of power it appears to have worked very well as Catherine was elevated from being a commoner to being THE power broker on the throne of one of the most powerful kingdoms of its day.

Here are some other talismans used by European royalty:

The friendship talisman

You wouldn't think the hard-nosed, pragmatic queen Bess would dabble in superstitions, but Elizabeth I had her share of protective amulets. She possessed an agate amulet which promised that she would always have at least one faithful friend. This amulet obviously worked because Elizabeth had a knack for surrounding herself with loyal advisors and spymasters throughout her life.

The religious talisman

A commonly worn religious talisman was that of the Agnus Dei portraying a flag and Jesus as the sacrificial lamb. The Agnus Dei was often made from the wax of a Paschal candle and was blessed by the Pope. It was carried to protect against flood, thunderstorms, windstorms and sudden death. Mary  Queen of Scots possessed two talisman stamped with the Agnus Dei and even took one to her execution. If you count a swinging ax as a sudden death, then this one didn't work so well for Mary. The great poet, cardinal Pietro Bembo gave the Duchess Lucrezia an Agnus Dei as a token of his secret love for her. In one of the many steamy letters to the Duchess, he wrote: *'The enclosed Agnus Dei, which I wore a time on my heart, you will deign to wear at night sometimes for love of me - if you are not able to wear it in the day - so that sweet dwelling place of your precious heart, to be able to kiss which one single time for a long hour I would bargain my life, may be at least touched by that circle which a long time touched the dwelling place of mine. Be well.'*

The health talismans

One of the most common talismans was a unicorn horn to protect against disease and poisoning. Unicorn horns were so expensive that some even cost the price of a small estate. Henry VII, Elizabeth I, Francis I, and Mary Queen of Scots possessed unicorn horns to ward off illness. (They were really overpriced narwhal tusks) Henry VII also possessed a serpent's tongue on a chain to protect him from sudden poisoning and illnesses. In ancient Malta, located off the coast of Italy, serpent's tongue were believed to be the tongue of snakes that  had been turned to stone. (They were really fossilised shark's teeth.) In the fifteenth and sixteenth century, serpent's tongues were suspended from coral trees, called languiers, and placed at the dinner table. Guests would grab a tongue and dip it into their wine to protect them from poisoning. Try this amulet only if you are dining with some suspicious house guests.

Talismans for commoners

If you couldn't afford a unicorn horn, then you would have to settle for carrying a mole's foot in your pocket. (just slightly nastier than a rabbit's foot) This superstition was recommended by Pliny the Elder in the first century C.E. and continued to be a common practice in England up until the 20th century. To cure toothache, people often carried a  tooth-shaped stone or animal tooth. These amulets cured tooth ache by transferring the disease from your tooth onto the stone. If you squeezed it pretty hard, maybe you would forget about the stabbing pain in your jaw.

Anne of Cleves use one that any commoner could use. She wore a crown of rosemary on her wedding day because it was believed to be a love charm. Judging by the speed at which Henry VIII divorced her, expectant brides might want to forgo this tradition.

Money talismans

Another common amulet was an alchemy coin called a 'thaler' which when carried would protect against disease and illness. The word 'thaler' became the basis for the word dollar which today ironically transfers nasty germs instead of protecting against illness.

Shew stones

Shown here is the purple crystal used to cure illness and predict the future. It was used by Elizabeth I's conjurer, John Dee who claimed he could see ghosts in it.

"Quick Useful & Effective Spells for the Seven Most Wished For Things"

Distributed through Ingram and available from all good bookstores or you can order it on-line here:

http://www.lulu.com/shop/sh%C3%A9-dmontford/quick-spells/paperback/product-18874554.html

Magick Magazine No. 9

WINTERFEST

Medieval Fair
Hawksbury Showgrounds July 6&7 2019

THIS YEAR WAS GREAT NEXT YEAR WILL BE GREATER

This is shaping up to be the BIGGEST and BEST event of its kind in Australia. All denominations and flavours are more than welcome from recreationists, to fantasy and steampunk. For those how have been the victims of religious discrimination at other festivals, **you don't have to hide your pentagrams.** For those who have attended The Abbey in Queensland. THIS IS BETTER... Bigger, better organised, friendlier and NO QUES!!!

WINTERFEST SYDNEY MEDIEVAL FAIR

Escape to Winterfest for a weekend of history and fantasy!

NEXT YEAR

Winterfest will be held at the Hawkesbury Showground on the first weekend of the winter school holidays 2020, on the **4th and 5th of July, 2020**. We are open **10am – 5pm** both days.

Winterfest is easy to get to, with free parking on site and a railway station only two minutes' walk away from the venue gates.

Join their mailing list to be sure you receive updates as we look ahead to Winterfest 2020!

From jousting, archery and combat to crafts, cooking and games, Winterfest offers entertainment to watch and activities to try. You can also browse the offerings of our carefully selected merchants. There's something for all ages:
- Participating Re-enactment and LARP groups
- Australian Medieval Combat (AMC)
- Entertainment & activities throughout the day
- Winterfest Costume & Cosplay competition

For a full list photo credit please go to the Winterfest facebook & website https://winterfest.com.au

Our editor, Shé D'Montford was there right next to Kevin Kelly and his bodhran drums

Look for the Winterfest logos to show you the way

History & Fantasy collide.

Anachronism abounds.

Stepping back into the past is so much fun for everyone.

FIONA HORNE ROCKS ON

Magick Magazine had the privilege of attending Fiona Horn's Spoken Word launch of her magickal manifesto "The Art of Witch"

Def FX also did a flying tour of one night only performances round Australia where Fi got to ge her good old rock on.

GIVE AWAY
Fiona signed a copy of the mag for one of our lucky readers. JUst go to our Face book page and tell us why you think "MAGICK MAGAZINE ROCKS ON" for your chance to win a little piece of Fiona Horne

No Conditions - you can enter as many times as you like! - Go for it!

If you miss Fiona like we do, you can keep up with what she is doing at her official website
http://www.fionahorne.com

Members of Qld Women's Power Coven enjoying the night-Including Shé, Fi, Ronnie, Nyx & Amy

Packing Out the House

THE PATHWAY TO THE GODDESS

The Camino Compostela - The Way of the Goddess
The Camino de Compostela was the original interfaith Pagan pilgrimage path. The Way of The Goddess following the Milky Way down to the sunless sea. The crocked path of self discovery and the path to Magick and miracles.

> *"Pilgrimage is relating to nature-to the sun coming up, to wondering if it's going to be too hot or if it's going to rain that day. When you walk, you think about your intention with nature and how we place ourselves in it. We are one with nature when we walk. Pilgrimage can bring up pain, inspiration, and empowerment."* Olivia Elliot

Later the Christians subsumed this odyssey path as Camino de Santiago, The Way of Saint James. The French alchemist Fulcanelli says:

> *"The Way of Saint James is also called the Milky Way. Greek mythology tells us that the gods followed this route to go to the palace of Zeus and the heroes as well followed it to enter Olympus. The Way of Saint James is the stellar route, accessible to the chosen ones, to the courageous, persevering and wise mortals."*

Christian Pilgrims have been travelling the road to Santiago on foot or horseback for over a thousand years and, at the height of its popularity in the 11th-12th centuries, over half a million people a year made the pilgrimage from all over Europe. Santiago de Compostela was one of the top three medieval pilgrim destinations (Rome & Jerusalem), with pilgrims flocking to embrace the statue of the Christian apostle James the Greater whose mortal remains are said to lie buried beneath the silver shrine in the Santiago cathedral.

Pre-Christian History
However, this path was trekked for millennia before Christian times. Sacred wanders from Pagan Greek, Roman, Celtic & Scandinavian traditions were known to follow the path laid out on the earth by the milky way, to lands end, Finisterre, where The Goddess would welcome them out into the ocean to be born again from her scallop shells. The Celts had a solar altar there to worship the setting sun. It was the gateway to mystical land of Tír Na nÓg, a land that knows no sorrow and where nobody ever ages, Land of Eternal Youth, where 100 years feels like a day. The Goddess who guards the way to this kingdom is Naimh. She rides the backs of the white horses on the waves. She is the most beautiful young woman, surrounded by a golden light, whose hair is the colour of the setting sun, and whose garment is the pale blue sky studded with stars.

The legend of Tir-na-Nóg says one can only reach the Island of Tir-na-Nóg in two ways; one must either receive an invitation from the goddess, or one must have walked the long hard road looking deep inside oneself. And when reaching Finisterra, you would receive your initiation in the name of the Hag, *Corella*. Her burial tomb is still there, so you can visit her anytime.

However the path seems to be even older than these traditions. The Camino follows the path of the Milky Way, along the Iberian peninsula (past the church of Santiago) towards Cape Finisterre (Land's End) the most westerly point on mainland Spain. Like other places with pre-Celtic origins, Galicia, on the path is full of megaliths, standing stones and prehistoric sites and some basic research revealed that many of the Christian cathedrals, shrines and holy places on the Camino were built on the site of more ancient temples. Masculine phalic spires were raised over the sacred womb like wells of the trail. Santiago de Compostela was no exception, with excavations revealing not only the remains of an older cathedral destroyed by the Moors but also a Roman temple and an even older Celtic well. Another famous Camino landmark, the Cruz de Ferro or Iron Cross, marks the highest point of the track and was originally the site of a Pagan monument.

The Saint James Controversies
'Santiago' is Spanish for 'Saint James', while 'Compostela' means 'path of the stars'. The official explanation for the city's origin is that in 835 AD, the secret burial place of St James the Apostle was revealed by a bright shining star twinkling over a remote field. However, further research shows that when Christian pilgrimages to the burial site began in the 9th century, this road of the stars already existed and had done for hundreds if not thousands of years! The Camino was a feminine empowerment walk down to the womb-like waters of Finnesterra, (Land's End) for millennia before the Christian patriarchy overlaid it with phallic spires.

St Junia The First Female Apostle
Even the Christianising of the place is open to controversy. The first female Christian Apostle was saint Junia. However she was not just the first woman, she was described as "First among the apostles," by St Paul. Even in her own day the giving of a woman first

place amongst all of the apostles, male and female, caused a controversy and so the apostle Paul wrote to settle this. Junia was referred to in the gospels as a woman in her own right, not as an attachment to someone else, or the wife of another. Junia had earned her title and position on her own merit. Yet, she has become the lost apostle, seldom spoken of. Additionally, She became transformed into Saint James on the Camino. Junia is suppose to have been buried where it is claimed that the bones of Saint James now rest. Her hagiography says she wandered from Spain, eastward along the Camino and over the Pyrenees into Europe to spread the gospel. They settled in Pannonia. (the Danube valley) After the death of her husband, Saint Andronicus, Saint Junia's is said to have wandered westward, back along the same path by which they had arrived, into what is now France and towards Spain where she buried her husband "under the stars" and later was buried there along with him.

St James the Moor Killer

The military Order of Santiago, named after James, was founded in Spain in the 12th century to fight the Moors. Later, as in other orders of chivalry, the membership became a mark of honour. This came about because in the 9th century, Spain was under Morrish control. They had erected a huge mosque and brought some of the bones of the prophet Mohamed there to create prestige and to anchor Andalusian Spain and the the Umayyad Caliphate firmly into the Islamic world empire. This resulted in two things. Firstly, the desire of the Islamic people to defend this outpost of the Caliphate resulting in Spain being strengthened into an important Islamic centre. Secondly, a vast number of Moslem people made pilgrimages to what was now a sacred site and centre to their belief system. Very cleaver of them! Though the reigning Moslems had an amicable existence with the Christian kings, who were granted their own state, the Papacy was not happy at the infidel intrusion so far into Europe . The Christian kings needed a reason to incite the rest of Christendom to war with the Moorish people in Spain to restore Papal control of Spain. The remains of the less popular female Saint Junia must not have held enough pulling power for the church to achieve this. So, suddenly. we find that the bones of Saint James were brought for a sacred burial to this ancient place of sacred burials. The chapel of the saints bones became known as in Santiago, (Saint James) Any person who was willing to fight for St James was granted absolution of all sins

Giovanni Battista Tiepolo St James the Greater Conquering the Moors
Wikkimedia Commons

upon their arrival at the church that housed the Saint's bones. They did not have to be a rich knight or nobleman to make this journey. If they had no money, and were still willing to fight, all they had to do was to be willing to walk the ancient Compostela to get there, then they would be treated as holy pilgrims and housed and fed along the way by other Christians. This would add merit to them in heaven and may even grant them a miracle. This mirrored and parried the Moslem claim. Christians from all over Europe poured in towards Santiago. They blazed new trails that connected with the Compostela. Today it is still possible to walk to the Compostela from many other places in Europe.

Scholars agree that James may not actually lay in Santiago. James suffered martyrdom in AD 44 in Judea. According to the tradition of the early Church, he had not yet left Jerusalem at this time. He never traveled to Roman Hispainia. It is not until this conflict began in the 9th century that any suggestion began that Saint James had been evangelising in Iberia, therefore his body would have had to have been brought to and buried on the sacred burial way of the Compostela. No earlier tradition places the burial of Saint James in Spain. A rival tradition places the relics of the apostle in the church of St. Saturnin at Toulouse; if any physical relics were ever involved, they might plausibly have been divided between the two. The tradition of Saint James' burial in Compostela was not unanimously accepted, and numerous modern scholars, following Louis Duchesne and T. E. Kendrick, reject it. Cheeky Kendrick says that *"...even if one admits the existence of miracles, James' presence in Spain is impossible."* Henry Chadwick suggests in his book that the Cult of James already existed in Spain, when it was thought to have been introduced to supplant the Galician cult of Priscillian, who was widely venerated across the north of Iberia as a martyr. He had been executed in 385 by greedy local bishops, not as a heretic.

Tradition states that Saint James miraculously rose from the dead to fight for the Christian army during the legendary battles of Clavijo and San Millán and was henceforth called "Santiago Matamoros" (Saint James the Moor-killer). The battle cry of *"Santiago, y cierra, España!"* ("St. James and strike for Spain") was the traditional battle cry of medieval Spanish Christian armies. This was central to the madness of Don Quixote. Cervantes has him explaining in his play that he is tilting at windmills for *"...the great knight of the russet cross who was given by God to Spain as patron and protector."*

The Cross of Saint James and the Shallop Shell
The symbol of the Order of Santiago was a sword with the hilt surmounted with a scallop shell. James' emblem was the scallop shell or cockle shell, and pilgrims still wear that symbol on their hats or clothes. The French term for a scallop is coquille St. Jacques, which means "cockle of St. James". The German word for a scallop is Jakobsmuschel,

Goddess symbols of the Gourd = Fertility & the Scallop = Birth & Rebirth overlaid with the masculine sword of war

EARLY DEPICTIONS OF THE GODDESS IN A SCOLLOP SHELL ABOUND

Above: Birth of Venus (Aphrodite-Greek) in a scallop shell. Roman Pompeii, 1st C A.D. Museo Archeologico Nazionale di Napoli, Naples, Italy. :The Birth of Venus

Aphrodite is born from the sea in the heart of a cockle shell. To her left is Hermes, holding his caduceus. Eros flutters by her side, and to the right sits Poseidon with trident in hand. Greek Attic Red Figure, ca 370 - 360 BC, Museo Archeologico Nazionale, Salonica, Italy.

Terracotta figure of Venus within a cockle-shell; 2ndC BC, Ruvo, Italy; British Museum.

The Triumph of the Marine Venus. Flanked by two cupids standing on dolphins, the goddess of beauty is seated in a sea-shell carried by two tritons. Dish handle; Gaul, late 2nd to early 3rd century AD; Louvre.

Birth of Aphrodite; Hermetic Culture, Egypt, 5th-6th century AD; Louvre.

which means "mussel of St. James"; the Dutch word is Jacobs schelp, meaning "the shell of St. James". In Danish and with the same meaning as in Dutch the word is Ibskal, Ib being a Danish language version of the name Jakob, and skal meaning shell.

Yet, predating this, Pagans associated the scollop as the symbol of The Goddess and a sign of rebirth. The Greek Goddess Aphrodite (Roman Venus) emerges from her birth in the sea in a scollop shell. The name 'Aphrodite' comes from the word "foam", aphros which implies more specifically sea foam. Hesiod calls her "the sea foam-born goddess" (Theogony, l.196) Aphrodite/Venus has been depicted in the scallop shell since pre-Christian times. The trademark Camino scallop shell is an ancient symbol for the setting sun and was a focus of pre-Christian Celtic rituals in Galicia long before the birth of James. The scallop shell is also a Pagan fertility symbol connected with The Roman Goddess Venus and the divine feminine.

The Witches of Galicia

However, mementos of women so powerful that they could fly, are openly displayed along the Camino, especially in the Galicia region. In the yards of private homes along the pathway there are statues of a woman with a long nose. The offical explanation is that these are a version of Mary. This is obviously not the case. They are described by the locals as yard witches and witches on broomsticks are available in most gift shops. These are very reminiscent of the statues of Aradia, the shining one, the morning

star, (Venus) the mother of fairies and protector of witches, often seen in gardens in rural Italy. Witches find Magick in aligning their lives with the cycles of nature, earth energies and the stars. In fact, the whole of the Camino from St Jean Pied de Port to Santiago de Compostela, is peppered with villages, places and mountain passes named after stars or after a trail of light, as if it were a stellar route, a route leading to a special destination - the field of the star. In Roman times, the road to Santiago was a trade route known as the Via Lactea or Milky Way. And today those stars can be seen everywhere – on signposts, in churches, on rose windows in the Gothic cathedrals, on the stone wells and monuments and on restaurant menus. And before the Romans came the Celts.

Today science is rediscovering what our ancestors knew thousands of years ago. They knew the earth to be a living organism. That its life force flowed through power channels, like blood through our arteries. They marked important power places on these energy channels with wells, dolmens and megalithic structures. They built their temples near nexuses of power, where the telluric currents of the earth met with the astral currents of the skies. Sacred places are where the manifestation of 'as above, so below' can be felt. Regardless of your religion this is what makes a place holy. Additionally, The Camino de Compostela follows the path of the sun from east to west across Spain, which from an earthly perspective appears to lie directly under the Milky Way. Both the French and Spanish sides of the Pyrenees are dotted with dozens of stone circles or cromlechs, dating back to prehistoric times. Studies have shown that these stone circles represent stars reflected on earth from the sky above and if viewed in groupings reveal the precise configuration of constellations in the same way the three major pyramids of Giza mirror the stars of Orion's belt.

Interestingly, the currents of Magick are felt so strongly here that even the students of Santiago de Compostela University refer to the grand library of the geography and history faculties as Hogwarts, because the magical linage of the area and of its resemblance to the huge library at Harry Potter's School of Witchcraft and Wizardry. The library was inaugurated in 1924 and is filled with glittering chandeliers, gilt-edged wooden shelves and elegant furniture. Visitors are also free to enter and look around.

Hogworts

The Pagan Bucket List

During a conference at Salamanca University in 1999, Juan José Ochoa de Zabalegui presented his hypothesis that the original pilgrimage towards the west of Spain, which later became the Camino de Santiago, originated with the people who built these stone circles in the Pyrenees. In de Zabalegui's study, he emphasises the widespread belief in the ancient world that both ends of the Milky Way possessed a star gate. He writes of a stellar cult dating back to the 6th century BC who believed there were two doors for the passage of the souls, a northern gate in the constellation of Orion, represented by the summer solstice, birth and descent into the body and a southern gate at the tail of the constellation of Sagittarius, represented by the winter solstice, death and ascent to the gods. The Camino de Santiago following the Milky Way to the setting sun at Cape Finisterre was quite literally an earthly re-enactment of the soul's journey from life to death. It therefore is believed to have been a death pilgrimage to ensure a good rebirth.

Metaphysically therefore, a pilgrimage to Finisterre via Santiago, whether Christian or Pagan, represents initiation and a return to the source or dwelling place of the gods. Icons of Saint James show him preceded by a dog as he travels the Camino towards the sacred field of the star. The band of the Milky Way passes through the constellation of the Great Dog containing the brightest of all stars, Sirius. Sirius the Dog Star is at its brightest in the lead up to the northern hemisphere winter solstice as the dying sun travels through Sagittarius, (the constellation associated with St James) at the time of year associated with death and ascent to The Gods/Goddesses.

The Hidden Camino

Louise Sommer, in her book *The Hidden Camino*, shows that the Camino has been hiding secrets, for centuries, that reach deep into the mysteries of ancient Europe. Museums and churches along the Camino are filled with pictures and illustrations of women! Not just any women, but women depicted together with huge towers; eggs; large silver crescent moons; serpents; portrayed as teachers and leaders; scholars and academics. They are present within every single church and museum. Except for The Virgin Mary and sometimes Mary Magdalene, all females were unnamed and unmentioned. The hidden secrets of the women along the Camino are congruent with the history of powerful women we have been taught to forget. Hypnotised to never ask questions about. This is the unconscious psychology behind the fear of women, why female sacredness has been demonised to suppress women and the matriarchal cultures, but also to create a division between women and men. Most of us have no clue just how many independent, powerful and intelligent women have existed throughout European history. Yet, wherever one looks around the world, this story seems to repeat itself. In Egypt, one of the most important Pharaohs was a woman (Hatshepsut); in the Bolivian revolution, one of the most important figures was an Ecuadorian woman, Manuela Saenz. The Sun God wasn't always a male, and the Moon God wasn't always a female. Women Vikings fought and plundered alongside the men; they had equality and rights not seen at anywhere anytime in Christendom.

European women in history have been reduced to 'romance and motherhood'. The Camino keeps a record of when European women were so much more. This all begs the question as to why was the church so determined to remove the power from the feminine. We will discuss this in a future article. Sommer surmises:

> *"We have amputated each other and in this separation, lost the connection to our innate spirituality and inner wholeness. We are not looked upon as whole human beings, but merely small limited shapes we are forced to fit into. Women who like to dress like 'a man' are being called transgender or butch. Men who wear certain colours are gay, all which is complete nonsense! Another example is how we judge how we define a 'real' man. Our innate spirituality and identity has been genderised on the premise of suppressing women, which also has caused us to lose the vastness and freedom of our being. It has all become external, instead of internal; our identity has been projected into shapes and norms, instead of an inner foundation of strength. A strong foundation with roots going deep into the earth, and strong branches reaching up into the sky. Learning from all these women and Goddesses along the pilgrimage, I started to realise the price we have paid, and are still paying, for the loss of this innate spirituality."*

The Camino as a Spiritual Journey Today

Many people believe that walking the Camino de Santiago opens them to life-changing personal and spiritual experiences powered by the energy from the Milky Way above and the millions who have trodden the earthly path below. There are many people whose lives have been completely transformed by this journey across Spain. Open-hearted love, overcome by tears of joy, wonder or gratitude are the soul's natural response to the incredible natural, architectural beauty and energy of the places on this track. Walkers experience goodwill, kindness, openness and warmth within the group of fellow travellers and from the communities transversed on this journey. It really is a magical journey to be a courageous mortal who returns to the source whilst watching the stars of the Milky Way twinkling overhead every night.

The question still remains: Why will you walk The Camino de Compostela? Is it because Santiago houses the bones of St James, St Junia or Mohammad? Pilgrims don't care. The site is ancient and sacred. It is full of power. Walking the path is transformative. It changes you. It doesn't matter which saint or god/dess you walk it for. If you walk this crocked and winding path Magick Happens!

Buen Camino! © Shé D'Montford 2019

YOUR PERSONAL INVITATION

If you would like to **JOIN US** there is a trip to The Camino happening for NH Summer Solstice 2020 which some of our readers will be taking. It is a 790 km walk starting from Lourdes, on the 1st June where we will meet the icon of the Black Madonna whilst it is making it own pilgrimage . Because there is filming, we will take 50 days to walk the trail which is only about 16km per day. If you can afford to take a month and a half for yourself, **It will be a transformative once in a lifetime experience** The Camino is free to walk but you will still have to pay your own airfares, accommodation and food - which is very reasonably priced.

PLAN & PREPARE - If you would like to accompany us please do some more research. People who have done The Camino are happy to blog about it online and there is a lot of advise & lots of guide books. Please see the list below to get you started.

Your editor, Shé D'Montford, has been invited to be part of a documentary about The Camino by The Starwalkers foundation. The foundation director describes its mission this way:

"Great change often comes from small actions of committed people working together for progress, and Star Walkers Foundation Inc. is a rallying cry to establish dignity and equal positions in society for women that are long overdue. As a foundation, our mission is to provide women the opportunity to embark upon a meditative pilgrimage towards healing, transformation, and empowerment. In June 2020, we will embark and document our first annual pilgrimage with 13 women from around the globe. Together these women will walk a deeply personal, physical, and spiritual journey along the ancient interfaith pilgrimage of the Camino de Santiago de Compostela ("The Way of the Stars") from France to Spain. Covering 500 miles in 50 days and forced out of their routine, comfort zones, and cultures, these women will be confronted with their strengths and weaknesses stripped bare to discover what makes each of them feel free, empowered, and independent. In gratitude, Olivia Elliott." Founding Director/Producer - Star Walkers Foundation Inc.- www.starwalkers.org

We are fundraising for this project. Even if you can't come with us it would be great if you could be part of making such a worthy goddess filled documentary. Because both Starwalkers and Shambhallah are charities any donation is tax deductible. If you would like to register to walk with us I am asking that you may find it in your heart to donate via the:

Fellow Travellers for The Goddess eventbrite link here https://fellowtravelersforthegoddess.eventbrite.com.au
or Donate directly via Paypal https://shambhallah.wordpress.com/donate

10 Reasons Why the Camino Is a Good First Long-Distance Pilgrimage Walk

1. You can take a **shower and sleep in a bed every day** for just $5/day.
2. You **don't need to carry any food** because there's restaurant meals available every few hours.
3. You **don't even need to carry water!** There's fresh piped drinking water about every 45 minutes.
4. **No need to carry your trash** with you for days since you'll pass a trash can about every 10 minutes.
5. As a result of all this, **your backpack could be as light as 1 kg** (2.2 pounds).
6. You don't need a map or navigation skills because the route is **well marked.**
7. The wide path lets you **walk side-by-side with your companion**(s), making for easy conversation.
8. It's flat, **easy hiking** nearly everywhere, with occasional gentle climbs/descents.
9. It's **extremely social.** There are lots of interesting people from all over the world you will meet.
10. You'll walk through 5-20 rustic villages per day.

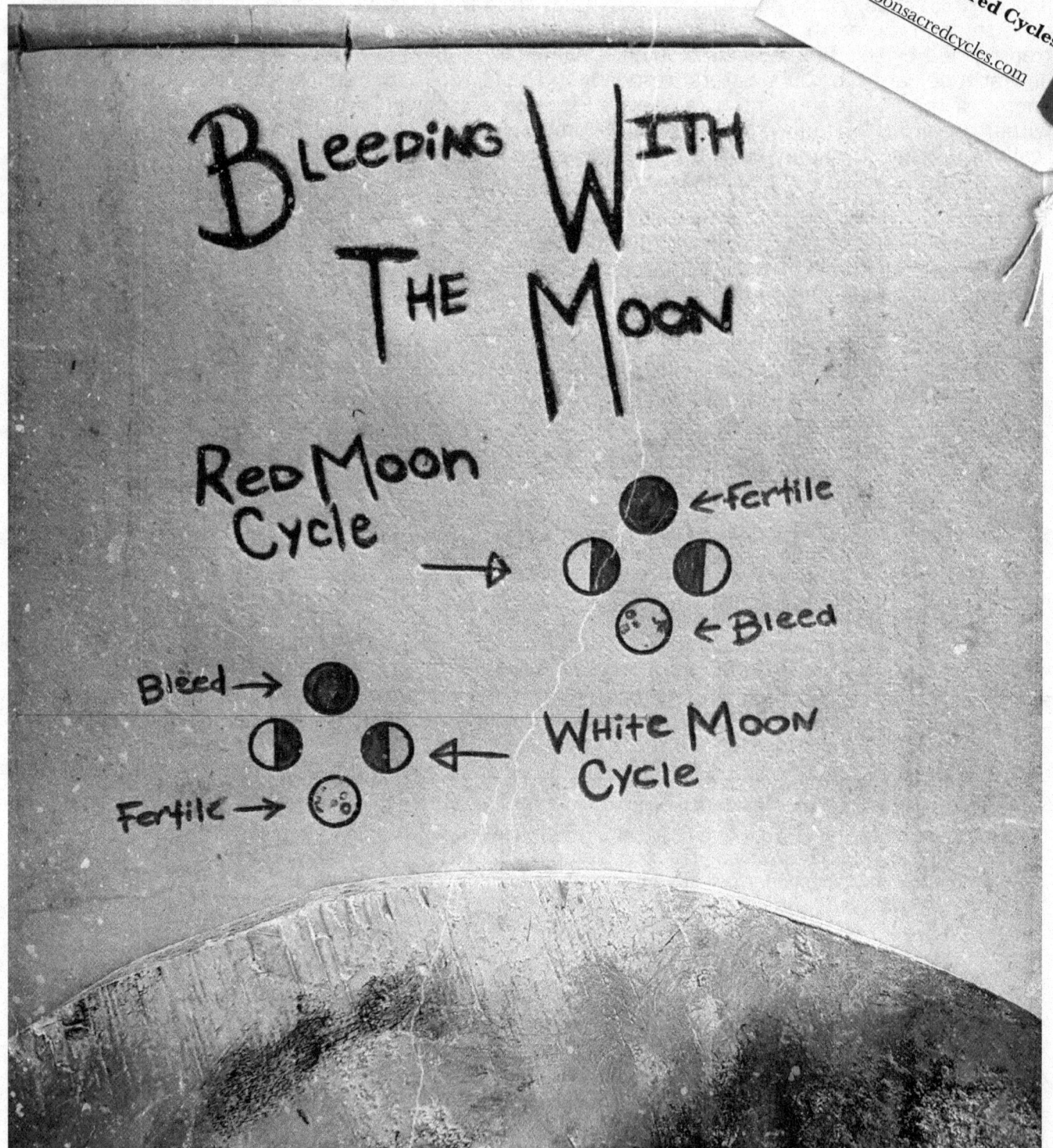

THE FERTILE MOON

BY ALICIA MEEK

Whether you are trying to become pregnant or avoid pregnancy, here are the facts according to the Moon. These facts will also be useful for any woman looking to reconnect with herself, her Moon, balance her hormones, regulate her period, or become healthy.

The wisdom of the Moon is finally back in style after a nearly 15,000 year suppression. Witchcraft & Womancraft are ever so connected to Her divine wisdom and timing. Her clock ticks inside each and every female body, even those without a womb.

The question is, how does the Moon affect my womb and the potential of pregnancy. To start the Moons' Cycle is 29 ½ days and the Menstrual Cycle is 28, sitting just inside the cycle of the Moon. Women will be within one of two main cycles of Moon & Womb, the Red Moon Cycle & the White Moon Cycle.

- When a menstrual cycle begins within the Waxing Phase, nearest to the Full Moon, and ovulating with the Waning, nearest to the New Moon, she is on the Red Moon Cycle. The Red Moon Cycle is associated with the archetype of the Wise Woman, for she is the shaman & the healer of her tribe. Her focus is collecting and passing on the ancient wisdom which was passed down to her.

- When a menstrual cycle begins within the Waning phase, nearest to the New Moon, & ovulating with the Waxing, nearest to the Full Moon, she is on the White Moon Cycle. This follows the natural cycle of the Earth, being most fertile with the Full Moon & akin to the Earth, ready to receive seed

Observing, during each Menstrual Cycle, which Moon phase you bleed with will give you the knowledge you need to either become or avoid pregnancy. What's more, this knowledge signals you, in advance, to your own internal Waxing and Waning phases, the condition of your personal health, upcoming hormonal changes and whatever else your unique cycle holds.

When a woman is on a **White Moon Cycle,** she is much more likely to fall pregnant. The reason being, the Full Moon is the best time to plant a seed on Earth, you are a part of Earth, and seed may be planted in you. A White Moon Cycle woman must be most aware of falling pregnant 5 days leading up to the Full Moon, as sperm can live in the cervix for up to 5 days, and an additional 3 days following the Full Moon. The, sometimes subtle, sometimes not, decrease in sex and happy hormones will mark the fertile phase over. Feeling into your body every day over lunations of New and Full will make you an expert in your own body, fertility and cycling, giving you in depth knowledge of what's to come.

A **Red Moon** woman will heed the same warning, though is reverse. She will be most fertile 5 days preceding the New Moon and 3 days following.

If you are Red Moon woman wanting to fall pregnant, or simply a woman looking to regulate her hormones to have a more predictable cycle, spend more time soaking yourself in Moonlight. The female body is programmed to ovulate / become fertile with the Full Moon and bleed when the Moon is dark. The Moonlight will reset, re-regulate, and balance your hormones to realign with Her, in a White Moon Cycle.

This may be basic knowledge for some women out there but this next one is likely not, and is where many accidental pregnancies are conceived. Have you heard of the Lunar Return Ovulation? The Lunar Return Ovulation is an ancient rule of thumb, each woman has the potential to ovulate a second time during her cycle when the phase of the Moon is the same as it was when she was born. So, if you normally ovulate with a Full Moon and you were born on a Last Quarter Moon phase, you have the potential to be fertile once more in a time you would otherwise not expect to be. Though if you were born on a Full Moon phase, then this Lunar Return Ovulation would not be a worry.

The lunar effect on the Menstrual Cycle and fertility is finally beginning to be recognised by science and the medical community. We live in a time where ancient knowledge is slowly being proven by scientists, statistics and Doctors. As women, we have the ability to be ahead of the game by tracking, caring for, and listening to our own bodies. You are the expert of your unique experience in your body, and you can use that expertise to be aware of your fertility and so much more.

VIKING WEDDING

CHANNEL 7'S EXTREME WEDDINGS

It was my great privilege to perform a Pagan Viking Wedding for Tiarne & Daniel and for it to be filmed by Channel 7 for their up-coming prime time show **Extreme Weddings.** (Sept 2019)

The Pagan community helped with everything from mede to outfitting to staging and Joth-Jar re-inactors helped the groom with a ban of Viking warriors to help prove his worthiness of the hand his beautiful norse princess. See our story on them on page .

Hopefully this will help bring public awareness to the fact that we need to stand up for our right to be married legally and religiously according to our deeply held beliefs.

For more information on **Legal-Religious Pagan Weddings** phone Shé D'Montford on 0402793604   and from outside Australia +61402793604

http://www.shedmontford.com/magickal-weddings.html

SPIRIT FESTIVAL 2019

Chameleon Spirit Festival is soon becoming one the biggest spiritual event on the Gold Coast. The inaugural event was a huge success with over 30 stalls and free talks and demonstrations all day. The second Chameleon Spirit Festival is shaping up to be even bigger and better will be held on Sunday the 11th of August from 10am-6pm. Chameleon New Age Salon is a huge 500 square meter sanctuary located in the heart of Surfers Paradise. They offer a large variety of services including Yoga, Ayurvedic Treatments, Psychic Readings, Aura Photography, Hairdressing, Piercing, Clothings, Jewellery, New Age Products and much much more. This business is extremely progressive and in their 4th year of operating. Chameleon is hosting some of Australia's biggest spiritual authors including, Lucy Cavendish, Inna Segal, Adam Barralet, Cheralyn Darcey, Patsy Bennet and Shé D'Montford. If you have't already been to Chameleon do yourself a favour and come and visit the biggest, most beautiful spiritual centre on the Gold Coast.

SPIRIT FESTIVAL

SUNDAY 11 AUGUST 2019

10AM - 6PM

FREE ENTRY

Welcome to our second Chameleon Spirit Festival. This festival is all about bringing together our Spiritual Community.

Chameleon
NEW AGE SALON

Ph: (07) 5526 8368
Shop 4/3171 Surfers Paradise Blvd, Surfers Paradise, 4217
Web: chameleonnewagesalon@gmail.com

YOGA ~ READINGS ~ HEALINGS ~ WORKSHOPS

ASTROLOGY ~ TAROT ~ JEWELERY

FOOD ~ CRYSTALS ~ BOOKS ~ AND MUCH MUCH MORE

HERMETIC INVOCATION TO HELIOS GOD OF BRILLIANCE

Magick Magazine No. 9

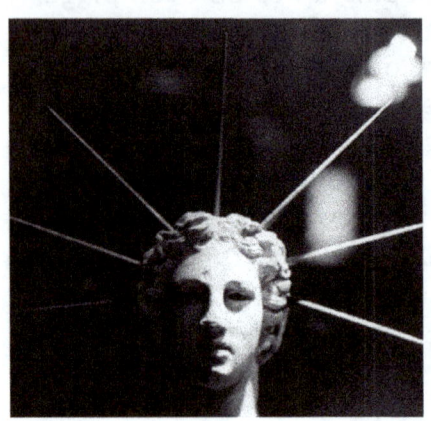

SUN

6	32	3	34	35	1
7	11	27	28	8	30
19	14	16	15	23	24
18	20	22	21	17	13
25	29	10	9	26	12
36	5	33	4	2	31

Know The God You Are Invoking:-

Sun: Helios, Apollo, Sol, Ra. The Sun can help a magician obtain harmony in his or her life by granting health, and reasonable amounts of money and friendship, and by showing him or her how to find peace through wisdom, all of which are essential to happiness and success. Conversations with this spirit are nothing short of inspiring, and they can teach one about several beneficial mystical secrets, including the miraculous art of healing.

Colour: Gold/Yellow.

Sent: Frankincense

Numbers: The numbers associated with Helios are 6, 36, 111, and 666.
This is because:
- Each row and column of the magic square contains six numbers.
- The square contains 36 numbers total, ranging from 1 to 36.
- Each row, column and diagonal adds up to 111.
- All of the numbers in the square add up to 666

In short, Helios was the god called upon for matters of intuition, inspiration, music, health, healing, athleticism, winning, prosperity, power and radiance. Apollo/ Helios was know to be very fond of human kind. He was a great lover, a great healer and a great friend. He was very proud when his devotees excelled in any field of human endeavour but hated pride and taught humility. Helios wants you to shine but not to be arrogant.He is the source of all power energy and electricity. Sun gazing has been central to many belief systems around the world. Many sages and scientist credit their "BRILLIANCE" to having sun shine in their eyes; including Tesla, Einstein and Jacob Boheme.

The Opening Ritual From the PGM XXXVI. 312 - 20

"Open up for me, open up for me, door; be opened, be opened, door,
Because I am Horus the Great,
ARCHEPHRENEPSOU PHIYRIGX,
Child of Osiris and Isis.
Immediately, immediately; quickly, quickly."
Tr.: R. F. Hock.

The Instruction: From PGM XIII. 7341077

EAST
Stretching out your right hand to the left and your left hand likewise to the left, say "A."
NORTH
Putting forward only your right fist, say "E."
WEST
Extending both hands in front of you, say " Ē."
SOUTH
Holding both on your stomach, say, "I"
EARTH -The point below PAST
Bending over, touching the ends of your toes, say "O."
MID POINT – straing in fornt of you - the here and now (The Point pf power is in the present moment)
Having your hand on your heart, say "Y."
SKY - The Point Above - FUTURE
Having both hands on your head, say "Ō"

"I call on you, eternal and unbegotten, who are one, who alone hold together the whole creation of all things, whom none understands, whom the gods worship, whose name not even the gods can utter. Inspire from your exhalation ruler of the pole, him who is under you; accomplish for me the what ever I request

I call on you as by the voice of the male gods, IEŌ OYE ŌĒI YE AŌ EI ŌY AOĒ OYĒ EŌA YĒI ŌEA OEŌ IEOU AŌ.

I call on you, as by the voice of the female gods,
IAĒ EŌO IOY EĒI ŌA EĒ IĒ AI YO ĒIAY EŌO
OYĒE IAŌ ŌAI EOYĒ YŌĒI IŌA

I call on you, as the winds call you.
I call on you, as the dawn."
(Looking toward East say) "A EE ĒĒ IIII OOOOO
YYYYYY ŌŌŌŌŌŌ"
"I call on you as the south."
(Looking to the south say) "I OO YYY ŌŌŌŌ AAAAA
EEEEEE ĒĒĒĒĒĒĒ"
"I call on you as the west."
(Standing facing the west, say,) "Ē II OOO YYY
ŌŌŌŌ AAAAAA EEEEEE"
"I call on you as the north."
(Standing looking toward the north say,) "Ō AA EEE
ĒĒĒĒ IIIII ŌŌŌŌŌŌ YYYYYYY"
"I call on you / as the earth."
(Looking toward the earth say,) "E ĒĒ III OOO
YYYYY ŌŌŌŌŌŌ AAAAAAA"
I call on you as the sky."
(Looking into the sky say,) "Y ŌŌ AAA EEEE ĒĒĒĒĒ
IIIII OOOOOOO"
I Call on you as the cosmos,
(Looking straight ahead into the middle distance) "O
YY ŌŌŌ AAAA EEEEE ĒĒĒĒĒĒ IIIIII"

Accomplish for me whatever I ask quickly.
I call on your name, the greatest among gods.
I call on you,
IYEYO ŌAEĒ IAŌ AEĒ AI EĒ AĒ IOYŌ EYĒ IEOU
AĒŌ ĒI ŌĒI IAĒ IŌOYĒ AYĒ YĒA IŌ IŌAI IŌAI
ŌĒ EE OY IŌ IAŌ,
the great name.

Become for me lynx, eagle, snake, phoenix, life
power, necessity, images of god,
AIŌ IŌY IAO ĒIŌ AA OYI AAAA E IY IŌ OĒ
IAŌ AI AŌIĒ OYEŌ AIEĒ IOYE YEIA EIŌ ĒII YY
EE ĒĒ ŌAŌĒ

CHECHAMPSIMM CHANGALAS

EEIOY IĒEA OOĒOE seven of the auspicious
names

ZŌIŌIĒR ŌMYRYROMROMOS"

"Ē II YY ĒĒ OAOĒ."

Helios Invocation from PGM XXXVI.211-30
for
SELF-IMPROVEMENT

x. Prayer to Helios:
A Charm to Restrain Anger and for Victory and for Securing
Favour

"None is Greater"

Say to the Sun (Helios) 7 times, and anoint your Hand with
Oil (Frankincense) and wipe it on your Head and Face.

Now the Prayer is:
"Rejoice with me, You who are set over the East
Wind and the World, for whom all the Gods serve
as Body-Guards at Your Good Hour and on Your
Good Day, You who are the Good Daimon of the
World, the Crown of the Inhabited World, You who
arise from the Abyss, You who Each Day rise a
Young Man and set an Old Man,
HARP ENKNOU PHI
BRIN TANTE 'NO' PHRI
BRIS SKY LMAS
AROUR ZORBO ROBA
MESIN TRIPHI
NIP TOU MI
CHMOUM MAO 'PHI.
I beg You, Lord, do not allow me to be Over-
Thrown, to be Plotted Against, to receive
Dangerous Drugs, to go into Exile, to fall upon
Hard Times. Rather, I ask to obtain and receive
from You Life, Health, Reputation, Wealth,
Influence, Strength, Success, Charm, Favor with
all Men and all Women, Victory over all Men and
all Women. Yes, Lord,
ABLANATH AN ALBA
AKRAM MACHAM ARI
PEPHNA PHO'ZA
PHNEBEN NOUNI NA ACH THIP...
OUNORBA,
accomplish this Matter which I want, by means of
Your Power."

Closing Rite From the PGM XXXVI. 312 - 20

"Close up for me, Close up for me, door; be locked,
be barred, door, until I open you again.
Because I am Horus the Great,
ARCHEPHRENEPSOU PHIYRIGX,
Child of Osiris and Isis.
Immediately, immediately; quickly, quickly."
Tr.: R. F. Hock.

The Instruction: From PGM XIII. 7341077

SKY - The Point Above - FUTURE
Having both hands on your head, say "Ō"
MID POINT - Strand in front of you - the here and
now (The Point pf power is in the present moment)
Having your hand on your heart, say "Y."
EARTH - The point below PAST
Bending over, touching the ends of your toes, say "O."
SOUTH
Holding both on your stomach, say, "I"
WEST
Extending both hands in front of you, say " Ē."
NORTH
Putting forward only your right fist, say "E."
EAST
Stretching out your right hand to the left and your
left hand likewise to the left, say "A."

© Copyright Rev. Dr. S. D'Montford, Saturday 7th August 1999 Gold Coast. Australia
Listen to the sound of the sSun recorded by NASA
https://www.youtube.com/watch?v=_fKkr7D807Y

THE DE LAURENCE MAGICKAL REVOLUTION

**The Truth about the Foundations of Western Magick
in the Late 19th & Early 20th Centuries**

Western Magick, Occult, Obeah and Voodoo all converge on one person at one point in time. It is sad that he has been largely overlooked or unfairly discredited by modern writers on the occult. I would like to pause to re-examine the ontological context and cultural contributions of L. W. de Laurence.

Who Was Lauron William de Laurence ?
Handsome, successful, wildly wealthy and innovative, L. W. de Laurence walked his talk and was more responsible than any other for making magick accessible to popular Western culture. L. W. de Laurence (March 20, 1868 - September 11, 1936) was an American occultist, hypnotist, teacher, author, and publisher of esoteric and occult texts, primarily through De Laurence, Scott & Co. of Chicago.

Prior to his publishing career, de Laurence was a lecturer on and demonstrator of mesmerism and hypnotism. During the early 1900s the *De Laurence Institute of Hypnotism and Occult Philosophy* and *Suggestive Therapeutics,* gained, public and professional, international acclaim with students from around the globe. During this period he became an A.M., Ph.D., LL.D., an instructor of hypnotism, psychology, and related studies at the American School of Psychology; in addition to being a *"student of the Orient in Practical Psychology, Metaphysical, Alchemy, Cabala, Occult and Natural Philosophy,"* and the credited author of the then industry standard *"Medical Hypnosis," "Practical Lessons in Hypnotism and Magnetism."*

He, personally, was the author of over 80 original works as well as being a publisher for other occultists. L. W. de Laurence wrote many texts which are still being reprinted today. His was the first and largest dedicated esoteric publishing house. Think Llewellyn combined with HayHouse. De Laurence became a very successful business man. His company became a huge global concern, selling millions of books and tarot decks. He also was the worlds first and largest business to supply magical and occult goods by mail order. In fact, de Laurence was a true pioneer in the mail order business. He was so successful that 125 years later his business, founded in the early 1900's, still exists today. Any good marketing course teaches his mail-order sales techniques. Although it has been said that his company has fizzled out, it still run out of a business front located in Michigan City, Indiana. With such a powerful presence in the world, we might ask who was this mighty occultist, and what was this company, that wields so much sway through such subtle means.

All prophets had a prophet. Buddha came out of Hinduism, Jesus blended Judaism with Buddhism, Mohamed blended Bedouin culture with Christian ideals, and 20thC occultists had Dr. L. W. deLaurence. Before Crowley, before Mathers, before Blavatski, before Waite, before Rhonda Byrne, before J.K. Rolling, there was Lauron William de Laurence. These radical occultists were able to show the way only because they had the elevated view from the vantage point of standing on de Laurence's shoulders. De Laurence published much of his work a decade before the famous names began writing on the occult. He co-authored with his fellow Chicago resident, the respected William Walker Atkinson. These books have become the basis of most modern western occultist traditions. For instance The central philosophy of Crowley's A∴A∴, "Scientific Illuminatism" was a catchy rewording of de Laurence & Atkinson's 1902 *"True Superior, Consecrated Science, and Spiritualism."*

Changing the World & Founding Belief Systems
It is by no means an overstatement to claim that the works of de Laurence, publisher of practical occultism, fomented the development of Pan-African mysticism, Black Nationalism, and Afro-Caribbean traditions. Even changing the way traditional practices were performed in Nigeria and Ghana. Historians universally acknowledge that De Laurels

L. W. de Laurence's officious faux-Old English writing style has been plagiarised by Waite & Crowley. He has been accused of pirating Waite's Tarot & Mathers/Crowley's Goetia, yet, the truth is that both Mathers & Waite were notoriously terrible with money & had shopped their manuscripts to many occult publishing houses. De Laurence was the largest esoteric publisher of his day. So of cause they would have approached the de Laurence company & most likely struck a deal, as there has never been a legal suit against him for a breach of copyright.

De Laurence, half smiling, whilst paying his token fine.

writings found their way into many of the Afro-Latino traditions. Reprints of the more popular titles are still currently available in Spanish language editions. His concepts were so integrated in to western Voodoo, (Voudo) Hoodoo and Obeah, that these traditions would not exist in their present form if it wasn't for his work. His books were hugely so popular in the Bahamas, West Indies, and the Caribbean Islands that it is hard to tell what magick looked like on these islands before they were integrated with the writings of de Laurence. His books were accused of empowering the common people so much that they could create riots and political unrest. The truth is that the governing class no longer felt safe from the justice of the common man. They were so scared by this wave of empowerment that all de Laurence stock and publications are banned in Jamaica. According to the most recent regulations of the Jamaica Customs: "*All publications of de Laurence Scott & Company of Chicago in the United States of America relating to divination, magic, cultism or supernatural arts...*" are prohibited from entering the country to this day! This includes de Laurence's entire catalog of books for mystics, together with all of his "*....Materials Accessory to the Pursuit of Mystic Study.*" This is an enormous amount of censorship as de Laurence provided hundreds of books and thousands of magickal accoutrements like incense, novelties and curios to millions of eager customers around the world. "*Despite its illegality, the practice of the de Laurence form of Obeah is still common in Jamaica, making it an integral part of Jamaican heritage.*" www.expeditionjamaica.com/topics/culture-and-religion/item/8-de-laurence-in-jamaica

David Metcalfe the editor-in-chief of 'Threshold: Journal of Interdisciplinary Consciousness Studies' suggests that it is "*amazing that this niche publishing company was able to produce practical results in the kind of cultural exchange that would later be central to the social engineering pursued by US International Cooperation Administration. The Chile Project, pursued by the USICA in the 1950's, sought to influence Chilean economic development through a graduate exchange program with the University of Chicago. It took 20 years for the effort, with established backing, to take effect. De Laurence was able to achieve an influence on the culture through a popular catalog of occult curios in approximately the same time span.*"

For those who would scoff at the magick popularised by the prolific output of Lauren W. de Laurence, it would be good to remember that the material in the books themselves have had a widespread, and often unnoticed effect on our contemporary culture. The methods of magick expounded by Harry Potter and the ancient truths expounded by "Time Magazine's Most Influential Person of the 20th Century," Rhonda Byrne, in her book "The Secret" have a lineage that lies in de Laurence's mail order mysteries that changed the face of global society, and deeply affected the racially charged geo-political climate of the 20th century. If one wants proof of the curio catalog's promise to teach powerful secrets of "*the mysterious influence of one human mind over that of others,*" it seems that affecting the fate of nations from a small office in Chicago isn't a bad start.

The Original Order of The Black Rose
L. W. de Laurence was the first person to run a registered magickal order in the U.S. in 1906. It was not masonic in structure or order, like many successive magickal orders, including the Golden Dawn, O.T. O and Wicca, and therefore was approved. Its structure was a cross over between what is now recognised as Voudo (Voodoo) and The Spiritualist Church. Though Blavatski had been running the Theosophical society since 1875, it was not officially incorporated until 1907 and not recognised officially in the U.S. until 1934. The Rosicrucians received recognition in the U.S. in 1915. It should be remembered that The Agape Lodge of the O.T.O., which many consider to be the first magickal order in the U.S. was not established in the U.S. until 1935, some thirty years later. The O.T.O.'s origins, through Theodore Russe, were directly Masonic, but because its degrees and workings were virtually identical, it was considered to be a clandestine lodge by the Masons and struggled to gain approval in the U.S., a country based on Masonic ideals in a time where the Masons were very powerful. Similar problems plagued The Order of The Golden Dawn. It did not have a temple in the U.S. till 1977, nearly 70 years after de Laurence.

De Laurence's occult order, the *Order of the Black Rose*, was eclectic and egalitarian. It admitted people from all social casts, races, creeds and genders. Its teachings were a blend of Elizabethan occult and eastern tantric techniques. In structure, it was more similar to the Hellfire Club in the U.K. in the 1700s. On 12 November 1912, Chicago police raided de Laurence's temple at 3340 Michigan Ave., arresting de Laurence, his wife Pauline, and others present, based on a complaint from a member Augusta Muerie. Newspapers reporting on the raid and subsequent trial focused attention to the claim that most male members were *"Negroes or Indians"* and female members were *"white women"* and that the cult was engaged in lurid activities, including nudity, and forays into the dark arts. Further, it was reported that the *"chief deity of the temple was found to be a regular cigar store Indian, which was the focus of the devotions and meditations."* Muerie went public to the newspapers before the trial, alleging that de Laurence *"practiced black magic and dressed in fantastic* (eastern style) *clothes"* and would *"throw himself into a trance and do strange dances of the Orient"* and that his wife and office assistant named Sadie Pyle were *"mediums for strange messages and advice from the spirit world."*

For all of this negative publicity, the only thing the court could confirm from witness statements was that Augusta Muerie had been told after going through the "weighing in" process, which involved stripping in a closed, private, mirrored closet, that de Laurence had remarked something to the effect that she was *"too fat to be an angel."* The courts explain to Augusta Muer that this insult did not breach the law. The post office inspectors returned "evidence," i.e. mail-order stock and de Laurence books seized during the raid, confirming that de Laurence, was not guilty of sending drugs and immoral literature through the mail. De Laurence was ultimately cleared of all accusations and was fined only $15 in municipal court for disturbing the peace by holding public inter-racial meetings, the cigar store Indian was confiscated and the temple was effectively disbanded. He reopened the order one week later, under the new title of "The *Order of the White Willow."* No action was ever brought against this "new" order by the police.

The Order of the White Willow eventually evolved into the American Catholic Church, a church composed of congregations which individually separated from the Roman Catholic Church, officially founded by Joseph René Vilatte in the U.S. It appears that this may also be a Gnostic lineage of Wandering Bishops of the Syrian-Malabar Lineage through the Church of Malabar in India via Kooran. In 1930 de Laurence was consecrated and created a bishop of this church by the Spiritualist, Arthur Edward Leighton, who was an Olympic hockey star and son of the Pre-Raphalite artist Edmond Blair Leighton. De Laurence's consecration helped influence the rise of the black spiritualist churches and the firm integration of Catholic saints with the Lwa in contemporary Voudo traditions, as in 1936 the year of his death, de Lawrence consecrated the first bishops for these churches, including Thomas B. Watson of New Orleans.

Unfounded Accusations of Plagiarism
There is not enough evidence to support the claims of plagiarism by de Laurence. In fact, under the most superficial gaze, we can see that many, many individuals have plagiarised de Laurence's writings without due credit. Most importantly, no litigation has ever been brought against de Laurence for breach of copyright. Additionally, the oft sited copyright loophole between the U.S. and London during that era could not be the reason for lack of litigation. It should be remembered that de Laurence sold books all around the world including Europe, and especially London. Customs did not impound his books for copyright breach in Europe. If a claim could have been made on the grounds of plagiarism then the London publishers would have done so on their own soil. The lack of litigation speaks very loudly in the defence of de Laurence, that there was no breach as the rights to the works had been on sold to him by either the authors or the publisher.

Modern literary historians unfortunately have fallen in to the trap of re-quoting internet summations that only look at publication dates and do not understand the publishing industry and its common practises from the era. It was common practise for writers and publishers to resell their works to multiple publishers in different countries. Indeed that practise still exists today. De Laurence reprinted many works by authors who had already been published in Europe, one of which is the oft mentioned "Lesser Key of Solomon" (The Goetia) 1906, by Mathers and Crowley, published by de Laurence in 1916. The friendship between Crowley and Mathers ended in 1905 when Mathers expelled Crowley from The Order of the Golden Dawn. Coincidentally, this is also about the time that Crowley self-published this work without Mather's permission. About 10 years later, Crowley writes about Mathers being in a deplorable financial state several times. He makes mention of his reselling his writings and even pimping out his own wife. If you were going to resell an esoteric manuscript, and try to get back at your co-author/editor, wouldn't you want to sell it to the largest esoteric publishing house in the world and leave his name out? Mathers, being who he was, would have expressed his vehemence at de Laurence if he felt it had been appropriated in the way Crowley had. However, Mathers remains silently content. This appears to be bourn out by the fact that in the credits where de Laurence takes credit as the editor and stresses that this is the:

Only Authorized Edition Extant.

WARNING. The student is warned, and most seriously admonished, to forbear from devoting his time to a study of cheap and inaccurate copies of this book which we understand are now being offered for sale. The price at which this book is sold is unquestionably a small one, and those who obtain it for less run the risk of becoming confused by studying a book which has not been properly translated and edited. This book has been published under the editorship of Dr. de Laurence, who, without doubt, is more competent for a task of this kind than any living man.

The Lesser Key Of Solomon
GOETIA
The Book Of Evil Spirits
CONTAINS TWO HUNDRED DIAGRAMS AND SEALS FOR INVOCATION AND CONVOCATION OF SPIRITS, NECROMANCY, WITHCRAFT AND BLACK ART.
TRANSLATED FROM ANCIENT MANUSCRIPTS IN THE BRITISH MUSEUM, LONDON
Ceremonial Magic
Only Authorized Edition Extant
Published Under The Editorship Of
Dr. L. W. de Laurence
Member Of The Eastern Order Of Sacred Mysteries
de Laurence, Scott & Co.
Chicago, Ill., U. S. A.

"Only authorised edition extant."

It is ironic that Crowley, with his unauthorised version, that he published without Mathers' permission, calls de Laurence a *"Yankee Thief,"* yet, in his books on hypnotism, de Laurence had been publishing about many of the subjects that Crowley wrote about even the "True Will," and "The Sun," Crowley's central catechisms, for a decade before Crowley began writing. Students of Crowley's will be very familiar with these central concepts, written by de Laurence a decade before Crowley began writing on the topic.

*"The fourth table is of the Sun, and is made of a square of six, and contains thirty-six particular numbers, whereof six in every side and diameter produce one hundred and eleven, and the sum of all is six hundred and sixty-six; there are over it divine names, with an intelligence to what is good, and a spirit to what is evil, and out of it is drawn the character of the Sun and of his spirits. This being engraven on a plate of pure gold, Sol being fortunate, renders him that wears it renowned, amiable, acceptable, potent in all his works, and equals him to a king, elevating his fortunes, and enabling him to **do whatever he will**. But with an unfortunate Sun, it makes one a tyrant, proud, ambitious, insatiable, and finally to come to an ill ending."*

The Great Book of Magical Arts - L.W. De Laurence 1908 -34 reprints to this day

The Other Oft Quoted & Far More Interesting Accusation, Is the Case of the Rider-Waite Tarot

About Pamela Colman-Smith & the De Laurence, Scott & Co. Publishing House.

Pamela Colman-Smith, nicknamed "Pixie," was a very cute, half-American, half-Jamaican woman who was raised in England. Coleman-Smith spent much of her childhood between Jamaica and Britain, and went on to study art in New York as a young adult. Much of her early creative work, including writing and illustrating books, was centred on Jamaican folklore, especially the Anansi Stories that inspired Neil Gammon's "American Gods." She would also go on to work in theatrical design. She was a lesbian and an early feminist who became involved in the suffragette movement. Additionally, Coleman-Smith was already an author in her own right. She was indeed a highly sought after illustrator for children's books and governmental war posters. Additionally, she worked for the literati of her day, people such as the poet William Butler Yeats, Bram Stocker, whom she called "Uncle Bramy," commissioned her to illustrate their work. Above all, she was a visionary artist who is best remembered as the illustrator of the Rider-Waite Tarot, though she received no acknowledgment or credit for it until 1938, when literary historians began to write about her. Waite never acknowledged the importance of Coleman-Smith's work. In the book written to accompany the cards, he failed to mention her by name, saying only that a "young black woman artist" had illustrated them upon his instructions. This dismissive attitude is inexcusable as they were equal members of the fraternal Order since 1901. Pamela had been a full member of the Order of the Golden Dawn right along with the better known members such as William Butler Yeats and Florence Farr. She was a founding member of the Golden Dawn before Arthur Waite caused his faction. Coleman-Smith originally met Waite through the 'Hermetic Order of the Golden Dawn' occult organisation, in which they were both members. Together, they would create one of the world's most popular tarot decks. Many tarot historians believe that the lion's share of the credit for the deck actually belongs to Coleman-Smith for the artwork and the authorship too. Waite admits that he only carefully controlled the creation of three cards: *"I saw to it that Pamela Coleman [sic] Smith should not be picking up casually any floating images from my own or another mind. She had to be spoon-fed carefully over the Priestess card, over that which is called the Fool and over the Hanged Man."* In contradiction to this, letters survive in which Waite sends Coleman-Smith to the British museum to make sketches from an Italian tarot deck from the 1400's on display there with permission for the collector . and in this letter Waite asks Colman-Smith for her interpretation of the meanings of the cards.

But if you hadn't previously heard of Pamela Colman Smith, you're not alone. Coleman-Smith's story sometimes gets missed out of tarot histories, and her name was left off most editions of her tarot deck until recently. But she certainly was a fascinating figure. If you're interested in learning more about her we will be running an article on her for the next issue.

Why would Waite always down played Coleman-Smith's contributions? Additionally, what reason could Waite have for going so far as to later dismissing this deck as his own creation? What could the possible motivation be for neither of them really wanting to take credit for the deck?

COMPARISON BETWEEN THE SOLA BUSCA TAROT & COLEMAN-SIMTH'S ARTWORK

Seven of Swords | Queen of Cups | Ten of Swords | Three of Swords

The Sola Busca Tarot Copy
The deck that Colman-Smith spent days viewing and sketching copies of in the British Museum is called "The Sola_Busca Tarot." The Sola Busca Tarot is the oldest Italian deck of cards in the world, and were named after their last owners, Count Sola and Marquis Busca. In 1924, the Ministry of Public Education recognised the value of this complete collection and its illustrations, and bought the rights to it and claimed first option to buy it – which it exercised in 2009, when the deck was put up for sale. The cards are currently kept at the Pinacoteca di Brera, which in 1971 had already acquired the Brambilla deck, a set of late-Gothic cards made for the Duke of Milan. The Sola-Busca is a fine collection of miniatures coloured with tempera and gold. Traditional subjects are replaced by characters from ancient Greek and Roman history and two biblical villains Nimrod and Nebuchadnezzar. The suits show allegories and scenes of daily life. The symbolism draws hermetic/alchemic culture from the late 1400's. The artwork has been attributed to Nicola di Maestro Antonio and coloured by Marin Sanudo. The Sola Busca Tarot is the only known deck with dynamic figures on all cards for four centuries where the preceding "Marseilles Decks" only have numerical features on the suits. Colman-Smith's finished tarot illustrations are almost identical to these originals.

De Laurence Published Tarots

The 1919 Yellow Deck

1936 Round & Four Colour Decks

De Laurence's "Square Yellow" tarot deck with the Coleman-Smith artwork first appeared in 1916 just 6 years after the release of The Rider-Waite Deck with de Laurences own booklet called "The Tarot." De Laurence had previously written about the tarot in his books but not in his catalogue. "Kabalistical Key of the Tarot," was a 60 page booklet, previously written by de Laurence. However, it has been speculated that the uncredited book "The Key to the Tarot" a.k.a. "Oracles Behind the Veil," that later accompanied the de Laurence Coleman-Smith Decks was Pixie's original unedited notes to Waite on her studies of the "Sola Busca Tarot" and her interpretation of their meanings. These facts comprise the most likely scenario.

Additionally, it is likely that Pamela Coleman-Smith, who was orphaned and who could not receive her inheritance from her uncle until 1919, would have eagerly sold her rights to de Laurence. If Coleman-Smith has sold her work to de Laurence, out of necessity or spite, why would she still be unwilling to put her name on it? It should be remembered that the art work was a direct copy of a museum piece that was privately owned and therefore encumbered by far greater copyright issues inherent in reproducing an exact copy of it, than there would be by reselling the work to an overseas publishing house. The copyright for The Sola-Busca Tarot, being privately owned and being in a private collection, belonged to the owner of that historical deck. The owner was never credited nor compensated, so that is likely why neither the artist nor the author were quick to lay claim to the reproduction.

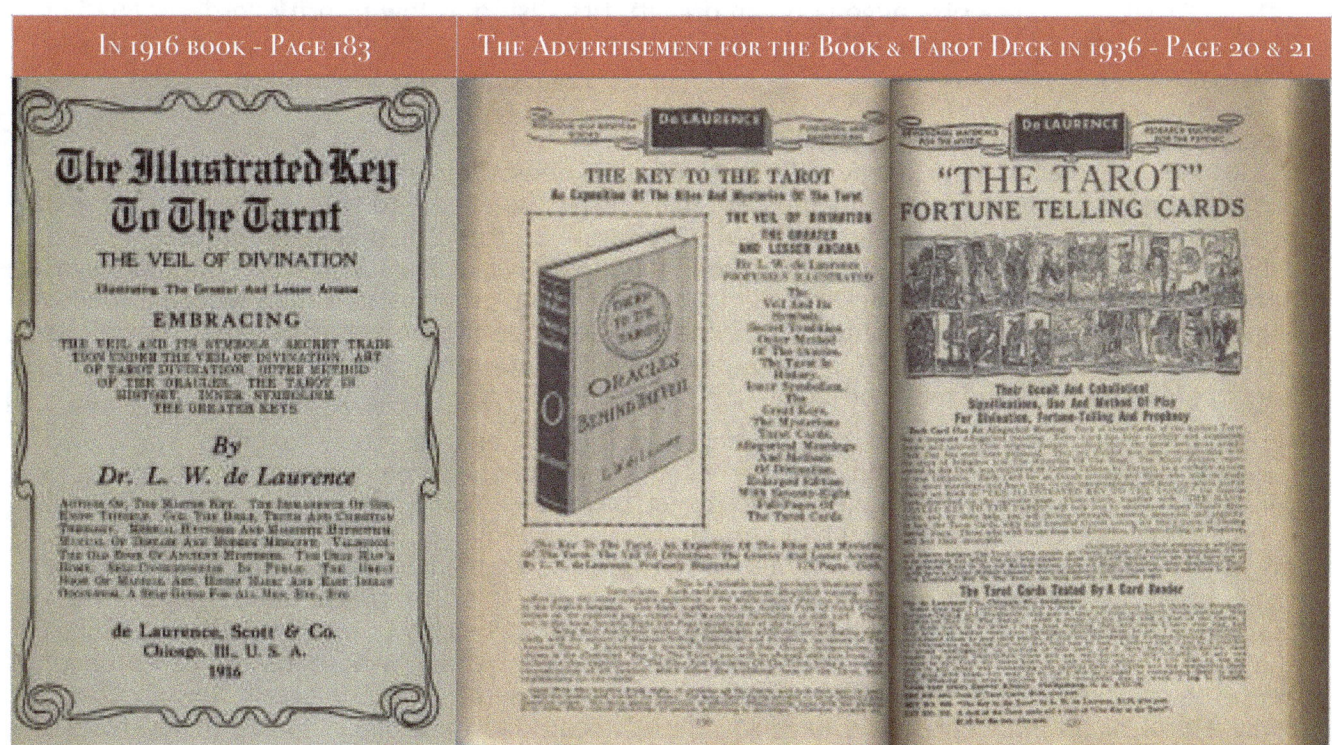

In 1916 book - Page 183

The Advertisement for the Book & Tarot Deck in 1936 - Page 20 & 21

Many people believed that Coleman-Smith wasn't paid for her artwork by Waite, and that invalidates all successive copyright claims. This is apparently not true. According to an interview with Mr. Kaplan of US Games, "*Pamela Colman Smith sent* [a letter] *to Alfred Stieglitz in 1909 or 1910 telling him that she had just done a big job of 78 illustrations for very little money. That was the Rider-Waite Tarot deck."* A work for hire is a work created for another person, for which you are paid in exchange for relinquishing claim on any rights to the work. If Coleman-Smith had not been paid, it would possibly call into question the chain of copyright ownership of the Rider-Waite Tarot in Europe. Since she was paid (even if it was 'very little'), she and her heirs had no further claim on the cards in Europe. However, She was within her rights to resell the art and her other contributions to another publisher. AS was A.E. Waite. What make us believe that Pamela Colman -Smith would have been inclined to enter into an arrangement with de Laurence?

She had a background in publishing herself, before the arrangement with Waite.
Her uncle Theodore Smith, had a book store and her maternal grandfather was the first to publish the Swedenborgian papers in the States. Additionally, she published her own magazine called "The Green Sheaf" and sold limited editions of her own prints and taught print colorisation to others. Colman-Smith also expanded from publishing to bookselling. She was no stranger to the industry. It must be remembered that she spent much of her childhood in Jamaica. When she was in Jamaica as a child, from about 10 to about 20, she became aware of Obeah, she wrote that it was important to her and she invented an Obeah character called for her stage act. Under the pseudonym Gelukiezanger, Colman-Smith would dress up and tell "West Indian Folk Stories" at private parties. She later published these stories as "Annancy Stories" (1899). It should be remembered that Obeah and Voudo are essentially belief systems based upon the writings of de Laurence. De Laurence was idolised Jamaica at that time and and still is idolised there today. This even though she was brought up as Swedenborgian with her family very involved in that church in New York and England. she converts to Catholicism in 1911. But what type of Catholicism, It is never stated that he is a roman Catholic. Even after her conversion she is not a typical Catholic. In an interview just after her conversion, she states that the first time she went to Ireland is when she first saw fairies and pixies, and became aware of Celtic spiritualism. Throughout her later years she ran a boarding house for old priests in Cornwall. (Please see our article on Crowley's Death in Cornwall.) So the Catholicism that she converted to was very different. It should be remembered too that de Laurence was a bishop of the American Catholic Church - a Gnostic linage. There are just so many little things, in belief system and practise that tie her to de Laurence.

This deck remains one of the best selling items in the de Laurence catalogue. Also worth noting is that the tarot got a huge boost in priority first listed as low priority "order # 697" in 1919, all of the way to "order #20," by 1936 with a giant two-page spread on pages 148 and 149.

Moden Magickal Amnesia & Arrogance
It astounds me that modern magicakl groups want to deny their heritage, claiming that they are the only true one or ancient arcane heritage or that they came to their understanding and practise from 'one' direct divine mystical revelation or that the heavens opened up and showed the universal truth and power to them only. However, it is easy to trace the language, phrasing and methods used back to de Laurence, from organisations like Wicca, Voudo, Obeah, Spiritualism, Gnosticism, the OTO and the New-Age movement in general. As well as to individuals considered to be ground breakers like Atkinson, Waite, Mathers, Crowley, Cannon, Hall, Bardon and many others.

My point is this, no one has the right to say that there is only one true magickal way, (even though de Laurence did) The admonition to be silent to avoid the 'wolves in sheep clothing,' (a phrase which several later occult groups lifted from de Laurence almost word for word, who himself got it from Aesop) serves to conceal the origin of their knowledge or to prevent discussion that might reveal what they don't know. If you can't discuss it with anyone then they have you. We grow when we share and discuss. Our communities get stronger producing stronger, more magickal individuals. I recently had the unfortunate experience of trying to discuss 'things they didn't understand,' with a long established magickal order, whose tenets of 'silence' keep them locked in the past. If any speak out, it is a case of 'The Emperor's New Clothes:' 'only a fool or an innocent would dare say there's really nothing there.' Well, in my foolish innocence I have created this magazine to share information and spark discussion. We love hearing back from you and if you can teach me something new as well then we both win and are evolving the world magickally.

Young, Velo de Laurence, pictured right, took over the running of his family business before his father's death in 1936. After over 125 years of changing the religo/magickal landscape and individual psychology with occult mysticism, plus scandal, successes, and mail order innovation, one thing above all is certain:

If history is any indication, De Laurence, Scott & Co. is unstoppable.

© Shé D'Montford 2019

A Partial Bibliography of de Laurence Writings

- A Message to All Mystics.
- A Self Guide for All Men
- Albertus Magnus Egyptian Secrets,
- Clairvoyance and Thought-Transference; Auto Trance and Spiritualism; Psychometry and Telepathy 1888
- Crystal-Gazing & Spiritual Clairvoyance: Behind the Veil-The Trance Sleep
- Raphael s Ancient Manuscript of Talismanic Magic.
- Dreams, Visions, Omens And Oracles.
- God, the Bible, Truth and Christian Theology
- Goetia the Book of Evil Spirits.
- Great Book Of Magical Art.
- Healing. Telepathy, Clairvoyance, Spiritism And Bible Contradictions
- Hypnotism, and magnetism, mesmerism, suggestive therapeutics and magnetic healing .
- Hypnotism: A Complete System of Method, Application and Use
- Magic, black and white - Charms and counter charms. Divination and demonology among the Hindus, Hebrews, Arabs and Egyptians.
- Persian And Chaldean Magic.
- Practical Lessons in Hypnotism and Magnetism
- Seals And Talismans; Their Construction, Powers And Influence.
- Self-Consciousness in Public: How to Control Your Emotions, the Problem and Cure of Self-Consciousness
- Spiritual Clairvoyance.
- Superstition in all ages - A dying confession
- Talismanic Magic. Occultism.
- The Bible Defended: The Holy Scriptures Upheld
- The Cave of the Oracle: The Great White Brotherhood.
- The Great Book - book1.
- The Great Book of Magical Art Book.
- The Greater Key of Solomon.
- The Illustrated Key to the Tarot: the Veil of Divination
- The immanence of God 1888.
- The Master Key.
- The Mystic Text Book of "the Hindu Occult Chambers"; the Magic and Occultism of India; Hindu and Egyptian Crystal Gazing; the Hindu Magic Mirror
- The sacred book of death, Hindu spiritism, soul transition and soul reincarnation.
- The 6th & 7th books of Moses the Wonderful Magical & Spirit Arts of Moses & Aaron.
- White and Black Art for Man and Beast.

Was the historic 15th century **All Saints Church**, located above the village of Clovelly, in Devon, the real final resting place of Aleister Crowley?

DID ALEISTER CROWLEY FAKE HIS OWN DEATH ?? TWICE ??

Aleister Crowley was infamous for many things, one of which was faking his own death for a month. In 1930, Aleister Crowley worked with his friend Fernando Pessoa to fake his death at the *Boca do Inferno* near Lisbon. Crowley left a sad note about heartbreak at the top of a dangerous rock formation, the implication being that he had jumped to his death. Pessoa, the celebrated Portuguese poet, followed up by feeding suggestive ideas to the local papers concerning the occult symbols that Crowley had used to decorate his note, and telling them that he had seen Crowley's ghost the next day. The papers ran with it, and announced Crowley's suicide. Some weeks later, Crowley arrived unannounced at an exhibit of some of his paintings in Berlin. It is assumed that he intended his disappearance to be much longer but could not resist the posthumous adulation of an art gallery showing of his own works.

Officially Crowley died 14 years later aged 72, on 1 December 1947 at Netherwood boarding house, Hastings, East Sussex, England. Netherwood, as the last resort for Aleister Crowley was a remarkable Hastings guesthouse. A lot of people think he died impoverished, this is just not the case. Around the middle of the last century Netherwood was a prestigious, bohemian, age care facility, to politicians, scientists, intellectuals and radicals, allowing them to be able to live independently of family or hospitals, and there were not too many of that style of facility in those days. It was expensive, paid for by the dues from his chartered organisations, including the Ordo Templi Orientis and donations from A.`.A members. Crowley's appetite was good and visitors were expected to bring him delicacies, like caviar, good wine and oysters. He was living very well. He still traveled quite frequently to London and to see his lover Deirdre and his son. He was in remarkably good health, given his earlier lifestyle choices and his age. He only recorded a mild worsening of his asthma, for which his doctor persisted in prescribing him heroine. Though Crowley claimed to not want this treatment he did not stop. Netherwood was also where the master magician supposedly spent his final years, playing chess, injecting heroin and receiving an impressive cast of visitors. Crowley writes of being board to the point of not talking to most of his visitors, whom he felt were dullards, who only wanted something from him. Despite Crowley's epithet of being the "wickedest man in the world", he was by no means an outcast. He rubbed shoulders with the great and the good of the age, including authors Ian Flemming, L Ron Hubbard and Aldous Huxley and even being intimate with the mother of a future U.S. first lady, Pauline Pierce, mum to Barbara Bush. He is known to have cooperated closely with British intelligence services during the Second World War and there is even a rumour that he invented Winston Churchill's famous "V for Victory" sign. Despite his association with the upper echelons of society and a life spent traveling the globe, Crowley chose to spend his last years in relative isolation.

Toward the end, he was "vigorous and his appetite was good," both great signs of recovery. The only indications of a man about to die were his letters to his acolytes for the previous 5 years, where he issues orders for his succession and then changes them and rechanges them. He prepared and then superseded his wills. Then without warning, Crowley summons Deirdre and his son to him, (the only people with him at his death) and is declared dead from bronchitis aggravated by pleurisy. Aleister Crowley's funeral was organised by a very few of his closest friends and associates. In accordance with his last will and testament, his cremation was instructed to take place during an occult ceremony at which magical rituals would be performed and occult verses read aloud. The chosen location was the Crematoria at Woodvale Cemetery in Brighton. However, there is no grave nor a memorial. After this, what was left of the Great Beast was mailed to the United States, where the remains were tipped unceremoniously in a back garden in New Hampshire. It is hard to believe that his fanatical U.S. followers would have made so little fuss about the arrival and interment of his remains in the U.S. To this day no one really knows where they are. Apparently, they were smashed in Karl Germer's backyard by his wife during a jealous rage under a non descriptive tree. But none of this can be confirmed.

Crowley's funeral took place on 5th December 1947. Only 4 days after his death. Remarkably quick for those days. It was attended by only twelve people. It was a closed casket. No one saw a body. Having solemnly processed through the grounds of Woodvale Cemetery, the guests congregated at the Crematoria, where it was said they read aloud from the Gnostic Mass, The Book of the Law, and the "Hymn to Pan" whilst Crowley's mortal body was turned to ash. After the funeral had taken place, the local Council declared the event a desecration of holy land and an act of abuse against the entire town. Just as with Crowley's first death, the media hype was huge. The outrage and terror of the local people of Brighton and Hove was immense. Christian services were hastily organised in and around the city in order to counteract the "malevolent forces" that the people feared may have been released by the acolytes of Crowley. An inter-congregational prayer meeting was held at St. Peter's Church, with around 10 clergymen from all Christian denominations attending and packed-out pews. According to the newspapers, Crowley was done with.

Until the 4th of April 2016 when The Cornish & Devon Post a weekly newspaper, published in Launceston, Cornwall, England, ran the following extract:

"ALEISTER CROWLEY, THE FAMOUS MOUNTAINEER'S GRAVE WAS DISTURBED ON FRIDAY. THE CEMETERY ATTENDANT WAS PERFORMING HIS NIGHTLY ROUNDS WHEN HE NOTICED A LARGE PIT ABOUT "SIX FEET ACROSS" AND RECALLED TO OUR REPORTERS THAT THE SIDES OF THE PIT WERE "EXTREMELY SMOOTH, LIKE IT HAD BEEN CARVED OUT WITH A GIANT CYLINDER BIT." AUTHORITIES ARE ASKING ANYONE WITH ANY INFORMATION ON THE IDENTITY OF THE THIEVES TO PLEASE CONTACT THE CLOVELLY CONSTABULARY AT +44(0) 1237 431256."

https://www.lashtal.com/forums/topic/aleister-crowleys-remains-stolen/
http://abrahadabra.com/aleister-crowleys-remains-dissapeared/ reported on April 4, 2016 at 8:25 am

Beautiful Clovelly, Devon, UK where Aleister Crowley may have entered into a secret secluded retirement of a Profess House, to focus on his personal Great Work for his sunset years

So I rang the police station and sent them an email - I was assisted by 2 officers a "Linda" and a Bea Stapleford the Media Officer - Alliance Corporate Communications & Engagement Department Devon & Cornwall Police and Dorset Police who assured me that though the incident was reported the police have no records as to the outcome. I also email the newspaper but have received no response.

So lets assume, for the sake of this argument, that Crowley, disappointed with humanity and disabused with the pettiness of the bureaucracy he could see forming within his order, decided to opt out of society, to have a peaceful demise.

It is not that far fetched. He hints at it in his letters to Germer in 1941:
"Note that the O.T.O. will probably have to be completely reconstructed. The temper of the New Aeon seems unfavourable for Lodges, and the "Secrets" are unintelligible to anyone who has not made a long study of the system. At present there are really

two sections; the rituals - up to Rose Croix; and the essays of instruction dealing with the one real secret. The ritual[s] corresponding with these were never written, except the Templar. So I rather expect that it will be up to you to devise some totally new method of communicating the real secret. This has, of course, been the actual procedure: I have simply used my judgement and spilt the beans to those whom I considered worthy. If the rituals, by some miracle, became widely worked, well. They are a splendid basis for the practical teaching."

In the above we can see, by this and his many other letters, that he has had enough. He is fed up with dealing with The Order and writing rituals that people don't understand and he is happily passing these responsibilities off to others; being Germer, McMurtry & Gardiner. Four years later, only 18 months before his official death, Crowley wrote this about his future plans in a diary entry regarding his will:

"Feb.7.(1945) to Saturnus re financial policy of O.T.O.
(1) A.C.'s copyrights belong to O.T.O. Each new book, or set of essays, or what not, is a direct gain to O.T.O. **To keep him alive & at work, with secretarial help, must be the first charge on the Funds whether labelled "Publication Fund" or otherwise.**
(2) Value of Grant. **If I die or go to** U.S.A., there must be a trained man to take care of English O.T.O...."(Gardiner)

If these wishes were adhered to a few would have had to know about Crowley's secret retirement; perhaps the 12 mourners, and, at the very least, Karl Gremer. If the report of the Clovelley Grave robbing is true then it would appear that Crowley went to Cornwall rather than to the USA. Why Cornwall? Here is a theory for you.

Retirement to a Profess House?

In 1911, Pamela Smith, the artist most famous for the illustrations of the Ryder-Wait Tarot, converted to what she called esoteric Catholicism. She had corresponded with Crowley after she became disillusioned with Arthur Wait and his Golden Dawn schism. After the end of the First World War, Smith received an inheritance from an uncle that enabled her to buy a house in Cornwall, an area popular with artists and bohemians. For income, she established a vacation/retirement home, very similar in type to Netherwood, for Catholic priests in a neighboring house. This is in the style of the Profess-Houses of Crowley's Ordo Templi Orientis.

One of his central goals for the Order was the establishment of Profess-Houses, which he also referred to as Retreats or Collegium ad Spiritum Sanctum. In the O.T.O. Manifesto, it is claimed that their exact location would be secret, known only to those who are entitled to use them but that they can be open to non-members. Among other things a Profess-House is for the purpose of being:

WHAT IS A PROFESS HOUSE?

- A place where *"members may conceal themselves in order to pursue the Great Work without hindrance"*
- *"They are also temples of true worship, specially consecrated by Nature to bring out of a man all that is best in him."*
- *"These houses are secret fortresses of Truth, Light, Power and Love"*
- *"Dignity and etiquette are to be strictly observed"*
- *"Brethren of advanced years and known merit" may retire at a Profess House.*
- In his writings before his death/disappearance, Profess-Houses seemed to be of far greater value to Crowley than local bodies.

This certainly seems to be the kind of establishment that Pamela Colman-Smith was running. It continued to be her main occupation till her death. She became very reclusive. She never married, and she herself died in Bude, Cornwall on 18 September 1951. Bude is only a few miles from the Clovelly Church yard that appears to be the true final resting place of Alister Crowley.

© Shé D'Montford 2019

The Landmark Haunted Bookshop in Melbourne Falls Victim to Religious Vilification

It has been part of the landscape of the Australian magickal community for so long we though it was always going to be there. It just goes to show that **THE WITCH HUNTS ARE NOT OVER.**

"I'M DEVASTATED, THIS IS SO SAD, I ALWAYS VISIT WHEN I VISIT MELBOURNE & ABSOLUTELY LOVE THE SHOP. NOW I DON'T THINK THERE ARE ANY DEDICATED OCCULT BOOK SHOPS LEFT IN AUSTRALIA THAT AREN'T JUST NEW AGE ORIENTED," ONE PATRON SAID.

THE COLOURFUL MR DREW SINTON IS A LEGENDARY FIGURE IN MELBOURNE & A MUCH LOVED PART OF THE AUSTRALIAN PAGAN / MAGICKAL COMMUNITY. HIS WONDERFUL INDIVIDUAL STORE OF CURIOSITIES IS A MUST SEE WHEN VISITING AUSTRALIA'S CULTURE CAPITAL

Drew Sinton, the owner of Haunted Bookshop which sells literature on the paranormal, ghosts, tarot, vampires, UFOs, fairies, demons, Paganism, witchcraft and ancient wisdom, has lodged a religious discrimination complaint with the Victorian Equal Opportunity and Human Rights Commission claiming he was refused a lease on a new shop because of *"the landlord's spiritual beliefs."* Haunted Bookshop owner Drew Sinton is in a dispute with his Buddhist landlord. Mr Sinton has traded on the paranormal and mystical for 22 years out of his popular bookshop in McKillop Street in the city's CBD. The shop is also the launching place for weekly, 'ghost' tour of Melbourne's haunted past that, along with the bookshop, won Mr Sinton the Lord Mayor's small business award. "I have never missed a rental payment nor had a landlord complaint the whole time I have been here," he said. Mr Sinton wanted to relocate his business, due to a drastic rise rent by his new landlord, to a new premises owned by wealthy businessman **David Yu** whose 'Ausvest Holdings' lists 41 properties in Melbourn. Mr Sinton contacted real estate agents JLL and inspected the property and applied to lease it, but was knocked back…

"Due to the landlord's spiritual beliefs he is not willing to put the Haunted Bookshop in his asset," the agent wrote to Mr Sinton.

When contacted by *The Age* and the *Sydney Morning Herald*, Mr Yu would not clarify his religious beliefs or the impact they had on the decision to refuse the lease, instead he handed the phone to Ausvest's general manager, Clare McArthur. "David is not going to provide any further comment on the issue," Ms McArthur told them.

MAGICK MAGAZINE

- HOW HYPOCRITICAL -

David Yu is President of the Buddha's Light International Society of Victoria, an organisation that last year won *Victoria's Multicultural Award for Excellence*. Plus, his Buddha's Light Society hosts Melbourne's annual Buddha's Day Festival which claims to promote religious tolerance… Yet, he is willing to squeeze out another minority group. This award should be stripped from him.

- HOW HYPOCRITICAL -

"So why was I really rejected because of your religious beliefs, Mr Yu?" asks Mr Sinton.

If Mr Sinton is not safe, then no minority group is safe in Australia.

!!ACT NOW!! Please write to your local politician and news service, protesting this. **!!ACT NOW!!**

Ask for Mr David Yu to not be allowed to be above Australia's anti-discrimination laws.

RE: 392 Bourke Street.

Harper, Alexandra (Alexandra.Harper@ap.jll.com)   Add contact   26/06/2019 3:47 PM

To: Haunted Bookshop;

Hi Drew,

I sent through the render, images of your shop and your website and unfortunately due to the landlord's spiritual beliefs he is not willing to put the Haunted book shop in his asset.

Are you available to inspect 179 Queen Street at all?

Regards,

Alexandra Harper
Senior Executive Leasing   M +61 407 052 070
Victoria

Level 40, 101 Collins Street, Melbourne   alexandra.harper@ap.jll.com
Australia, 3000   jll.com.au

A Facsimile copy of the disgusting email received by Drew Stanton on the 26th of June

THE MAGIC OF TOUCH

A few years ago I was privileged to visit an orphanage in Eastern Europe where strange diseases were attacking the children. The staff found this puzzling. If you walked through the rooms you would see these tiny tots gaze at you with a haunting stare. They looked more like shrivelled up old men and women. There was no sound of laughter, no sounds of children at play. They were slow to learn to stand and walk. Deep moans and long sighs were common. They had little appetite for food, became ill and died easily. The bewildered staff did not know what was wrong, and did not know what to do.

Then, some wise soul with a healthy mothering instinct made a suggestion. She suggested that some teenage girls from the local school be invited to visit the orphanage. She then instructed these girls to act like mothers to the children. She told them to pick the babies up, caress them and cuddle them.

As if by magic, a miracle occurred. The caressing and cuddling made a dramatic and healthy change in the children. It was so obvious from the first session that the girls were invited to revisit the orphanage again and again. Each time the tots were held, caressed and cuddled. With every visit the transformation continued. The children's posture improved. They lost their look of old age. They began to eat. They now smiled, gurgled and laughed. They no longer became ill so easily. They started to sparkle with life. It was apparent that these children had been starved of simple human physical affection.

This story makes me wonder: what is there about the sense of touch that can bring about such a miracle? Why is it our lives tend to become empty, hard, sick and indifferent without the touch of someone we love? Why do we seem to lose our sense of will and purpose without this loving touch?

The Physical Nature of Touch

Experiments in sensory deprivation have taken place with human volunteers. While physically confined, they were deprived of audio and visual stimulation and temperature changes. Such deprivation of normal sensory input led their minds to wander. They entered a world of fantasy. They began to hallucinate. Extensive and intensive sensory deprivation is not healthy for adults. It is not healthy for infants and children either. As long as we have a body, the world of sensory input is important to all of us.

Touch is probably the least explored of our senses, yet it may be the most important to our well being. Significantly enough, there is a close relationship between our skin and our nervous system. In the early days in our mother's womb, our body-to-be is composed of three sets of special cells. One set (mesoderm) will form our muscles and bones. Another set (endoderm) will form our inner organs such as the stomach, intestines and lungs. The third set (ectoderm) forms our skin and nervous system. Thus our skin arises from the same tissue as our brain. Skin can be looked upon as the outer brain or an extension of the brain. Its profuse sensory receptors are in full support of this idea. The skin is so full of nerves and sensory end organs that if we could see only someone's nervous system we would have no trouble outlining the complete shape of the body. We may wonder which has the most nerve tissue. Is it the cortex that covers the brain? Or is it the skin that covers the body?

Doors To Our Consciousness

The skin contains millions of sensory receptors. They are the doors through which the physical world enters our consciousness. How many types of these sensory receptors do we have? All told, we have five senses. The more obvious of these message receivers are our eyes, ears, nose and tongue. Even these four are really more than four. The eyes have rods in the retina to detect black and white. They also have cones in the retina to detect various colours. The tongue has sensory receptors for sweet, bitter, salty and sour. Our ears are able to hear a range of pitches and various intensities of sound. Yet, we are oblivious to very high pitches that can be heard by animals.

While we are inferior to some animals in the senses of sight, hearing, smell and taste, we more than make up for it in imagination and intellect. We assume a sensory edge over animals through our inventions such as the telescope, microscope, radio, television and so on. Smell may be the last frontier in our drive to surpass. It has been estimated that an Alsatian dog has one million times more sensitivity to odours than a human being.

Touch, the so-called fifth sense, may be the most complex. There are at least eleven distinct senses that compose touch. Under touch there are millions of sensory receptors in the skin. Yet, any one square inch of skin is different from any other square inch. The number of pain, heat, cold and other touch detectors will vary from one spot on the skin to another. We can see this as the sensitivity of our fingertips exceeds that of the back of our thighs.

There are some four varieties of the strictly tactile sense of touch. They range from light touch to deep pressure to pain. Again, their distribution in the skin varies as to type and quantity. If you place two

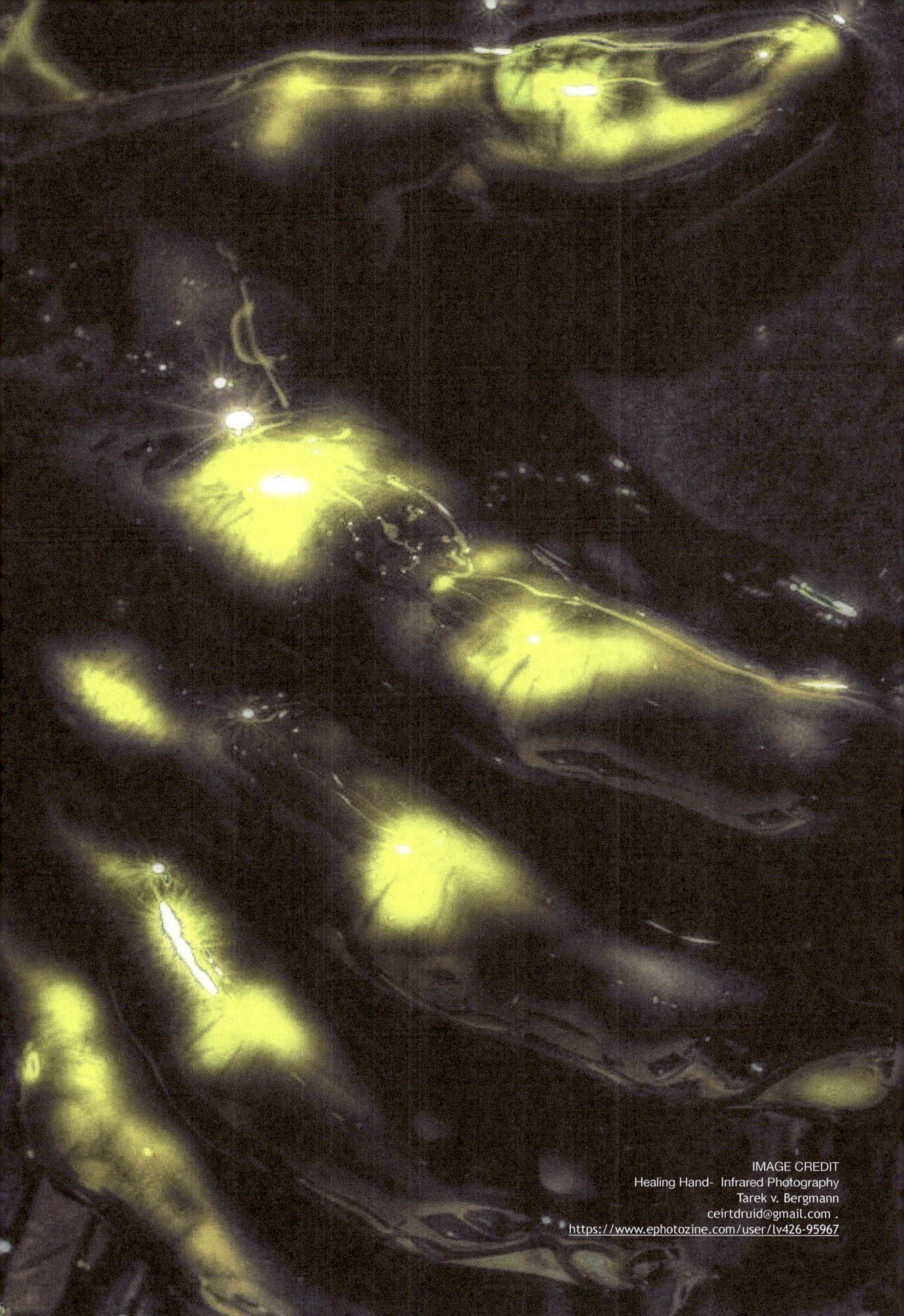

IMAGE CREDIT
Healing Hand - Infrared Photography
Tarek v. Bergmann
ceirtdruid@gmail.com .
https://www.ephotozine.com/user/lv426-95967

fingers an inch or two apart on someone's back, he or she may not be sure whether you have placed one finger or two. The human back has less light touch receptors than other skin areas. This is why patients are often very vague as to the exact spot of back pain. Oddly enough, it is in this lack of touch receptors of the back that we seem especially receptive to psychic impressions. According to some people our intuitive flashes come from our shoulder blades.

We find a more profuse distribution of tactile sense receptors in areas where our outer skin meets our inner skin (mucous membrane), such as our lips and nose openings. Also, our fingertips are rich with tactile receptors. Aside from being marvels of dexterity, our hands are our main medium of literally keeping in touch with the physical world. In a sense, hands represent our life's work. The use of our hands often marks our talents, our character and our culture. They have come to symbolise life itself. Through the use of human hands, guided by our brains, have come our great paintings, sculptures, writings, music and so forth. In science, hands have built cars, aeroplanes, rockets, radios, televisions, computers, as well as printing itself. And yet, perhaps the noblest use of the hand is to extend it in kindness to a fellow human being.

Therapeutics

The use of the human hand for therapeutic purposes goes back to ancient Egyptian times. It is claimed that the Egyptians felt a therapeutic energy (that they termed sa ankh) flowing from the fingertips. There are stories of the pharaoh holding daily morning healing sessions during which he made vertical passes, with his fingertips, up and down a patient's back. This, traditionally, was the beginning of hand therapy. The highly sensitive fingertips were approximating the insensitive human back.

The Greek Epidaurus tablets showed how the Ancient Greeks manipulated the spine of patients. Hippocrates, Galen and Soranus fostered this therapeutic approach. Hippocrates stated: "In all disease look to the spine." This is the early legacy of modern chiropractic practitioners. The chiropractic doctor finds an area of spinal irritation. He manipulates that area to reduce the irritation and normalise nerve impulses from the spine. The osteopathic doctor will do soft tissue manipulation of any lesions occurring at the spinal areas. The Rosicrucian technique is to apply the fingers and body's electromagnetic energy to the sympathetic chain ganglia that lie along the spine. Massage, digital acupressure and trigger point are other hand techniques that strive to improve human health.

Tender Loving Care

We should not overlook the benefit to a bedridden patient of tender loving care. I mean something quite simple such as turning and rubbing down the patient, propping a pillow, changing bed sheets, as well as giving a caring smile. Sometimes a sympathetic hand on a favoured brow is remembered longer and more endearingly than the most sophisticated treatment.

Aside from the therapeutic nature of touching, your body's sense of touch can be an avenue for you to help yourself. Stretching can be a tonic to certain touch receptors. A rocking chair is good for your nervous system as is a bath or shower, towelling yourself dry, and brushing your hair. Applying deep pressure on cramped muscles will relax them. We should also set aside time to expose our skins to the four elements: earth, water, air and sun.

We need to seek those experiences that are most wholesome, most uplifting, most creative and most beautiful. This includes being touched in an abstract sense by beautiful views, mellifluous sounds, delectable tastes, fragrant scents, as well as with the palpable touch of love. We need that human side to touch. A friendly hand on the shoulder during a crucial time is an uplifting and helpful gesture. Despair and tension can lock the shoulder muscles tight; massaging with the hands helps those muscles to relax. Similarly, how welcome is the firm and heartfelt handshake of a friend?

Talking and exchanging ideas is good, but friends and loved ones need more. They need the occasional physical touch generated from sincerity, genuineness and love. Get down on the living room floor occasionally and play with your children. Most animals follow their instincts and play with their young. It's fun and it's healthy. Even the most ferocious of animals have been known to become domesticated pets through large doses of affectionate care. Infants are in special need of this. Probably the most helpful thing to do to a withdrawn and frightened or badly disturbed child is to hold them, hug them and talk softly to them. In this way the boy or girl knows you are concerned. Such human contact through a loving touch can heal.

A "Non Touching" Society?

A judge who had hundreds of juvenile offenders and their parents before him made an observation that bothered him. In all of these cases he never saw a parent put a loving, protective arm around a youngster's shoulders. Is part of our trouble with today's youth due to a "no touch" society? Does the lack of the loving touch in our early years lead to emotional instability in our later years?

We should seek ways of applying the loving touch. This should be done with a genuine concern for another's welfare. When is the last time that you firmly grasped your partner as if he or she were your whole life to you? Your spouse may well be just that. Taking a child's hand as you cross the street tells them that you care enough to protect them from possible harm. The protective sense is no small matter. An evil man will think twice before interfering with a woman protecting her child. The protection of others brings out powerful forces in us for good.

Have you held any babies lately? Have you cuddled them? They need so much loving physical contact in those early years. Have you ever unashamedly hugged a good friend? Embracing friends, once the provision of Latin countries, is now commonplace. We are wise to do it. It's friendly and it's healthy. Also, make your handshake warm, sincere and definite.

Psychologists are realising that a "no touch" society is a sick society. It certainly is out of touch with the needs of our psychic and nervous systems. All this is not to say we should go around touching everyone indiscriminately. The protocols of our particular society will dictate the proper social limits of the physical touch. However, within those limits we can place a greater genuineness in our contacts. We can also touch people with our eyes, posture, voice, dress and good manners. We can particularly touch people with kind, sympathetic, understanding words; words to encourage and give strength. Such words help bring to fruition the seeds of greatness we see in each other. We can be touched by beautiful music or the sound of a voice from the heart. Beautiful sights, or the smells of nature and the taste of good food can also touch us in their own way.

To work the magic of touch there is one guide for us all. Let it always be from our heart. Let our heart touch people: "The nucleus of the brotherhood of men is the brotherhood of hearts." We are the most wholesome when our heart is expressed in our handiwork and when our own heart is touched by the handiwork of others.

After we are born we are left with no apparent physical attachments. But let us not fool ourselves. We all still need occasional wholesome elevating physical contacts. Our nervous systems, our emotions and our hearts thrive on it. The brotherhood of man demands it. We need to touch those we love and care for. They need our heart-felt touch. For, wherever there is genuine love and true concern, then there is a certain magic in the human touch.

- John Palo

Reprinted with permission from The Rosicrucian magazine. John Palo is a member of the Rosicrucian Order AMORC. Available as a digital download from www.amorc.org.au/rosicrucianbooks

PLUG INTO THE POWER OF THE UNIVERSE

For over 100 years, the Rosicrucian Order has made available its successful system of personal, home based study that gives you access to the fullest potential of being – physical, mental, psychic and spiritual. In simple weekly lessons you will find that our comprehensive approach makes your learning and personal development process easy.

We invite you to join with us and become part of a worldwide group of men and women dedicated to mystical knowledge in the widest sense.

You can harness virtually unlimited powers of insight, creativity, spirituality. You can attract people and events into your life, speed your body's natural healing processes, create harmony around you. And much more. All you have to do is learn how.

As the first step in discovering just how extraordinary you really are we invite you to read our free introductory booklet MASTERY OF LIFE - see it at: www.amorc.org.au or ask for your free no obligation copy by phoning: 1300 88 11 35 or email: mastery@amorc.org.au

AMORC

THE ROSICRUCIAN ORDER

THE ROSICRUCIAN ORDER IS NON-PROFIT, NON-RELIGIOUS, NON-POLITICAL

MAGICK

It is our aim to make this the best and most reliable resource for Magickal information internationally

Magick Magazine is a unique magazine for the magickal community

Its writers, artists, editors, marketing managers advertisers and production crew are all well respected members of the community.

There are no muggles or unethical people involved in this work.

The magazine will be posted on line in a flipbook format or you can order a full colour softcover book for $12.95 plus postage.

ADVERTISING RATES

Full Page		
A Dimensions 277mm (H) x 190mm (W)		$800
Half Page		
B Dimensions 135mm (H) x 190mm (W)		$400
Quarter Page		
C Dimensions 135mm (H) x 93mm (W)		$200
One-eighth Page		
D Dimensions 65mm (H) x 93mm (W)		$100
Banner Page		
E Dimensions 30mm (H) x 190mm (W)		$120
Classied Display advert		
F Dimensions 30mm (H) x 44.5mm (W)		$50
Classied Line advert		
G 3 lines or 30 words.		$30

VIEW ONLINE AT http://www.magick.org.au

Conditions of advertising: All prices include artwork design

☏ +61402 793 604

The WEEKLY Seer

'CROP CIRCLE' EPIDEMIC

An unprecedented surge of crop circle activity across rural England has seen the usually pastoral circles springing up in any available surface, from lounge room carpets to the hair of pets and humans. No suitable canvas is safe as residents across the affected areas can testify.

Mr. and Mrs. Vexed from Salisbury had a circle appear in their lounge room carpet as they sat reading. "It came as quite a shock," said Mrs. Vexed, "one minute there was our lovely carpet, then suddenly 'poof', and now look at it! I've tried three different firms of carpet cleaners, but no one can get rid of it. And of course, the insurance company says we're not covered for crop circles."

A number of men have had the circles appear in their hair and while the younger ones tend to be quite pleased with the effect, some older men are furious, especially when laughed at by their wives. Women seem to be mostly immune to the effect, perhaps because they don't often have hair styles which accommodate crop circling, or possibly because their use of hairspray and other products renders their hair immune to the phenomenon.

Crop Circle in Hair

Many pets have been affected, with cats suffering the most distress over the occurrence. We spoke to Hilda Lynx of Midsomer Bonkers who said, "My Claude went berserk when a circle appeared on his back. I had to drag him down from the curtain rod and sedate him, poor baby. I fear I will bear the scars for life."

Crop Circle on Cat

Scientists say there is no way to tell how long these phenomena will continue, and they call for the public to remain calm, cross their fingers and hope – or perhaps shave their heads as a preemptive defence.

Morganna with her warm humour is a well respected elder of our community. You can contact her on morganna13@hotmail.com

---

The Awakening
Imbolc Brisbane Witches
Masquerade Ball
Theme
EARTH WARRIOR
Dress as your Favourite creature, as we dedicate this magical night to our brothers and sisters of the earth.

contact Amy on 0428 418 097
email: mysticharmony@hotmail.com

AN ANCIENT STORY RETOLD THROUGH MUSIC

WENDY RULE: PERSEPHONE

Persephone, the new double-album from Visionary Songstress Wendy Rule is the culmination of over twelve years work, and although drawing on Wendy's musical journey over the past 2 decades, is unlike anything that she has done before. This beautifully evocative retelling of the Ancient Greek myth of the Goddess Persephone's descent into the Underworld and the subsequent grief of her mother, the Goddess Demeter, is a focused song cycle - almost like an opera - designed to guide the listener through this ancient tale of the cycles of Nature. With subtle textures that reference her early life as a jazz singer in her home town of Melbourne, and the trademark dark, gothic soundscapes and soaring vocals of her previous 7 major albums, *Persephone* is a unique 24 track journey through the realms of Life, Death, and human emotion.

Wendy sings in the voices of the 3 Goddesses that feature in the myth: the maiden Persephone who becomes Queen of the Underworld, her grieving mother Demeter, and the wise Goddess Hekate. A true labour of love, Wendy has spent the past five years travelling regularly to Greece to research and deepen her connection to the myth by visiting the ancient sacred sites associated with its worship. Since her first visit in 2014 she has also been learning the language in order to sing some of the tracks in Modern Greek, creating a bridge between the ancient and modern worlds.

For more information and to purchase Persephone, head to
www.wendyrule.com
Instagram: @wendyrule

THE END OF AN ERA

In loving memory of Luke Quadrelli
21.10.1968 – 9.5.2019

On Friday 24th of May we said our goodbyes to the amazing Luke Quadrelli, the owner of The Rendezvous Tea Room and the last of the mystical Tea Rooms. Luke was well known within the Brisbane community as one of the very best Clairvoyants. He had been doing readings since he was 17 years old. On this Friday I heard so many incredible stories at his farewell of how he helped and even saved people's lives. It was very moving, and he was a very humble man. I met Luke back in late 2012, he became a very dear friend and mentor. He taught me a lot of what I know about Tea Leaf Reading and much of what is in the first part of "The A – Z of Tea Leaf Reading" book, were the stories he told me of the old Tea houses in Brisbane and the many wonderful characters. There were many of these hidden gems around. Only the other day I heard a story from a lady that she had worked downstairs in The Pennies Building and she would see people sneaking up to the 5th floor to the Gemini Room to get a reading. This was back when it was illegal to do any type of psychic readings. You would ask to be careful with whom you told of these places. They would have a sign on the front door that would say something along the lines of, "We don't profess to tell about the future, it is for mere entertainment" At the same time in England you could actually get insured under the "circus performing act". It was still illegal to do any type of readings up until 2002 in Qld.

I started writing my book on Tea Leaf Reading and Synchronicities back in November 2012 and got in contact with Luke, as I had heard about him and his wonderful Tea Room. Not long after that he asked if I would like to work for him. It was a wonderful time, learning so much from him and working at the Rendezvous Tea Room. I ran my very first workshop in Tea Leaf Reading from Luke's shop. I suggested to Luke he should run his own workshop, but he didn't want to be in front of a whole lot of people. He said that I should teach the class. So that is how it all started. If was many years later before I realized I had written a book. It was a collection of Luke's stories and mine mixed with a dictionary of symbolic meanings. The A – Z of Tea Leaf Reading by myself, Kate Denning was published in March of 2019. Luke received his signed copy from me on Friday 26th April. He sent me a thank you message, along with congratulations, wishing me all the best and hopes of it becoming a best seller. This would be the last time I heard from him.

Luke Quadrelli died only 13 days after receiving my book. The irony of the timing is that this book might not have even come about if I had never met Luke.

I felt I had been guided to write Luke's story in the book and then I had the privilege of sharing a bit of that story at the farewell.

Now for the twister, I am now the caretaker for The Rendezvous Tea Room. I feel Luke everywhere, and I am keeping his legacy alive. I know Luke was guiding me (pushing really) to re-open his Tea Room.

Until we meet again Luke.

Love Kate

ANGEL - Spiritual protection, someone is watching over you. Love and peace. Connection with higher spiritual powers. Good news. The birth of something special.

Kate Denning is a modern day Mystic, talented Clairvoyant, and Spiritual Teacher/Mentor. Kate is highly skilled in the ancient art of Tea Leaf Reading, as well as Palmistry and Crystal Ball Reading. Kate offers one on one readings, psychic parties, workshops, and live talks.
FB: The Rendezvous Tea Room
Or The Spiritual Realm with Kate Denning
787 Stanley Street Woolloongabba Qld 4102
The A – Z of Tea Leaf Reading by Kate Denning RR $20
www.thespiritualrealm.com.au

LEAVE BEHIND YOUR PAST

I've spent the odd sleepless night worrying about the past and letting it influence my future. When it happens, I end up tossing and turning things over and over in my head for hours on end. I'm not alone in this as it happens to all of us at some time or another.

Sometimes we spend too much time worrying over the dumb things we've said to people we admire or stuffing up that all important job interview. Whatever the topic is, the past torments us at the most inopportune time. Dwelling on negative past experiences is painful, and if we hold onto that pain, it's impossible to move onto anything more positive.

At times like this, I remember the quote from **Ziad K. Abdelnour** a Lebanese-born American author

"Your past mistakes are meant to guide you, not define you."

Understanding what caused us to fail allows us to pick ourselves up and move on more quickly the next time things don't go our way. By integrating the lessons we learn into our lives, we can re-calibrate our reactions to events and create more meaning in life. Then we move beyond the old and into a newer, more awesome version of ourselves.

To stop dwelling on the past, forgive myself and live in the present I've created the following three tactics.

1. How do I feel about the mistake and what emotions am I focussing on?

Ask yourself this question and write down what immediately comes to mind. The first thing that pops into your head is the right answer. Anything else is secondary and has come from your ego and not your heart. True emotions come from our heart centre. So always take the first answer as the right one.

Don't be worried if the list is long and brings tears or anger to the fore. Allow that emotion to arrive and be curious about what it's trying to tell you. What we focus on, we create. We are all capable of talking ourselves into repeating a failure; just as we are capable of thinking ourselves out of it. Being curious allows us to get out of any destructive pattern of behaviour and belief.

Understanding our emotions enables us to create some perspective about failure and begin to forgive ourselves as we focus on letting it go.

Over many years working with Anxiety clients and by surviving it myself, I've learnt that this first step can sometimes be the hardest but is also the most rewarding.

Step TWO "Choosing to let it go" and THREE "Trust yourself and live for today" are detailed for you in my leaflet "How to leave the past behind" which has a bonus Infographic to print out and keep handy.

I'd love to hear from you about the newsletters and am available on Facebook https://www.facebook.com/groups/AnxietySupports/ and email mailto:tm@toni-maree.com.au to answer your questions.

Until next time; remember to stay awesome,

Toni-Maree.

If you'd like to know more about Toni-Maree you can find her at www.toni-maree.com.au While you're there, you might like to discover details of her upcoming "**Psychic Development**" and "**Happiness GPS**" programs.

LIVING VIKING TRADITIONS

JOTH GAR

The JorthGar branch of the New Varangian Guard concentrates its living history re-enactment primarily on the earlier Varangian Guardsmen of Viking origin, and their many exploits and accomplishments.

The original Varangian/Scandinavian Mercenaries that were given to Basil II in 988 CE (as part of a military and trade alliance), that formed the nucleus of the Varangian Guard and became his imperial bodyguard in the palace and on the battle field. We will cover up until 1066, where the composition of the Guard started to change, and the 'Viking era' ended.

These Mercenaries were originally from Sweden and had spent many years of service with Prince Vladimir in Russia, taking down rivals and helping him to subjugate his lands. They had become furious with the Princes 'incapacity to pay them correctly' and had demanded to be 'shown the way to Constantinople'. When Basil II had requested military aid from Vladimir to take down his rival Vardhas Phokas, Vladimir sent these 'unruly warriors' to help and rid himself of their financial burden.

As the treaty between the Rus and Byzantines was also a trading one, many Scandinavian, Slav and Rus merchants and artisans would have accompanied this force to Constantinople to take advantage of this. Some would establish trade routes, others would seek employment in the Byzantine army to help equip its soldiers.

Many of these warriors held fast to their traditional Pagan ideals and spirit, and derived inspiration from their ancestors and kinsmanship, even though their new employers were strongly Christian Orthodox. It is with these Varangians from which Jorth Gar derives its identity and focus. We also reenact warriors that returned back to their homelands after active service in the Guard, and have a strong civilian and family base within the group as a result.

Jorth Gar is based at the Gold Coast in Queensland, Australia. We can field the largest infantry battle force in Queensland and quite possibly Australia (real weapon combat) from any single group. This can be seen and experienced at shows like the NEMAS Armidale Easter Gathering and the Abbey Medieval Tournament, which are the biggest reenactment events in the southern hemisphere.

VIKING CULTURE DAY

Hosted by the Jorth Gar garrison of the non-profit New Varangian Guard Inc Living History Society. Sunday 11th August 2019, 8am to 3pm. Entry by Gold Coin. Held at 90 – 102 Curtis Road, North Tamborine QLD 4272 (Tamborine Mountain in the Park across from the Tamborine Mountain State Primary School, Cnr Curtis and Long Rds Eagle Heights).

Jorth Gar re-enacts the life and combat of the Viking and Eastern mercenaries that served within the Byzantine Empire, we also re-enact their Allies and Enemies of the Empire during the Dark Ages 988 – 1066 CE.
Watch Viking warriors battle with sword and shield, spear and axe! Have a go on the archery range – shoot at the Viking warriors! Come and walk through the Viking camp, learn about Viking lifestyle. See our Blacksmith at his forge. Displays of weaving, wood-carving, leather-craft and more! Hot food, hot and cold drinks available.

For further details, please contact Luke on 0448918901 or
Daryl on 0438 231 708.
Website: www.jorthgar.com
Facebook page for Jorth Gar:http://www.facebook.com/groups/103748892756/
Facebook page for Viking Culture Day: https://www.facebook.com/groups/450934854940791/

We are always recruiting for new members, and advise interested people to contact us (below) for more information, or to arrange to come to a training. Public are welcome to come and watch, but please remain at a safe distance when combat is underway, to avoid any injuries or problems. For more information, have a good look through our website.

NEPTUNES SCEPTER
Part 3 of our Erotic Pagan Fiction by DD Scarlet

Welcome to Salacia, Island of Sensuality.
Our Heroines have arrived at "Neptune's Haven," a bungalow style beach resort on an unspoiled island paradise. Here you can enjoy pristine beaches, hike through the mysterious jungle, paddle in tropical ponds by day or romantic moonlight swims at night. On Salacia, you will be treated to a sensual spa styled pampering each and every day and so much more...

https://ddscarlet.weebly.com

When they awoke the next morning Rainaa and Julia were escorted to breakfast, during which time another man, Rikiki serviced their bungalow. Their hosts then took them on a leisurely guided walk through the jungle, showcasing strange wildlife and striking fauna, secluded ponds and waterfalls and other panoramic wonders. Afterwards they were treated to foot spas by the pool where Mantou brought them more cocktails. And in the evening, after dinner they were fed more of the fertility potion.

The next day the girls began to feel a sensual warmth building within their bodies and they jokingly suggested that the fertility potion had aphrodisiacal qualities.

"No," Koa told them, "What you are feeling is your body's physiological reaction to the eggs growing inside of you." The girls just laughed at the notion and that evening they happily devoured more of the elixir.

The next day, however, Rainaa discovered her body to be hypersensitive. Her breasts were swollen and her nipples aching to be played with and several times she caught herself just massaging them as she descended into a whirlpool of lust. And there was a dull, continual throbbing in her pussy which was driving her insane! She urgently needed to be fucked, but although she was giving off all the right signals, Koa resisted taking advantage of her, instead seeming to just subtly tease her.

"I think they might be gigolos..." she suggested to Julia on the quiet.

"Do you think?" Julia responded.

"Well it would make sense... How else do you think they could afford to devote all of their time with us? I think they purposely get the guests as horny as hell and then offer to service us them at some extravagant rate."

"Well, hell... Where do I fucking sign?" Julia remarked making Rainaa laugh.

Then she conceded, "I know what you mean... I don't think I've ever been this horny in my life! I wonder what really is in that drink..."

"I wonder how much they charge!" Julia added before they both burst out laughing at their wicked train of thought.

That night, they were not expected to intake more of the fertility potion, but they were still accompanied at dinner, after which they returned to their bungalow where their hosts filled the large clam shaped bath, adding mineral salts and aromatic oils and petals before setting the jets on to the lowest possible setting; and lighting scented candles to further add to the romantic ambience of the space. Clad in their bikinis, they submerged in the bath, the bubbles erotically soft against their skin. The hosts devotedly sponged them which melted their muscles but at the same time stirred their repressed, raw desire. ...And then under sensually lowered eyelids, Rainaa turned to look at him, his face enticingly obscure in the candlelit room. Koa could tell that she had something on her mind and he asked her, "What's the matter, Rainaa?"

"Are you... are you gigolos?" she questioned.

"No," he answered her.

"Oh we don't mind..." Julia commented, "If you are."

"Julia!" Rainaa reprimanded her, making the men laugh.

"But we're not," Wakana told her.

"I feel so fuzzy..." Rainaa commented. "I think that potion..."

"What she means is she's horny," Julia blatantly informed them making Rainaa blush before again censuring her.

Again the men laughed before Wakana asked them, "Do you not like being horny?" The girls just stared at them.

Then Koa brushed his fingers across Rainaa's breasts and started lightly pinching her nipple, making her pussy throb unabashedly and she sighed in delight. "Can we hop in there with you?" he asked and they both nodded.

The hosts sat behind their guests with their legs wrapped around them and then tilted their heads back so they could kiss them as they continued to fondle their breasts. Rainaa sighed, her pussy aching desperately to be filled and she commented, "This is a bit like that poly fish orgy."

Koa smiled and corrected her, "Polygynandrous."

"Are you going to fuck us in the spa?" Julia asked quietly, happy to go with whatever was happening, and even Rainaa was too horny to object.

"No, we can't spawn with you tonight..." Wakana told her, shattering her.

"Why not?" Julia questioned.

"We may only spawn during the ritual of Salacia," Koa elaborated and when met by surprised and confused faces he confirmed, "We only fuck on the full moon."

"Why?" Rainaa queried. The girls couldn't believe their ears, they assumed that they had been fed some kind of love potion for three days straight and now that they were ready and aching to copulate like depraved bitches on heat they were being rejected..?

"Because we are Neptune's holy Sceptre and that is the discipline," Koa explained.

"Is this some kind of weird sex cult?" Rainaa asked.

The men laughed and denied the notion, "No..."

"Oh my God, I don't care if it is. I'm so horny right now..." Julia confessed, "I can't wait until tomorrow night."

Rainaa then turned to Koa, a sense of debilitating need exuding from her grey-blue eyes and he mercifully tucked his hand inside her bikini bottoms and slid his middle finger over her delicate, honey coated clit and petted it. Momentarily she puddled, modesty abandoned, and then she curled her arms around his biceps in a panic and held on tight, suddenly remembering that they were not alone in the spa. Koa kissed her ear and whispered, "Relax... I'm going to make you feel really nice, now." She looked up at him and he dropped his mouth upon hers, invading it with his tongue, before curtailing and whispering huskily, "And then tomorrow night we will fuck all night... I promise you. Would you like that, Rainaa?"

She opened her drug-laden eyes and quietly whispered, "Yes."

With the men in the bath the bubbles had risen high up under her chin, the heated, scented water erotically caressing her. Nobody could see her nipple dancing for Koa's skilled fingers, on his other hand gently touching her inside her bikini bottom. She could hear the wetness of their gentle kiss intermingled with Julia's soft sighs and then she realised she was sighing herself. They had been on double dates before, but never one like that one. Never one where they would be so completely seduced in such close proximity to each other.

Rainaa was beginning to find it hard to breathe calmly and Koa let her lips fall away from his, just wrapping them over hers every now and then. His large yet tender finger massaging her slippery clitoris was becoming uncomfortably wonderful... Almost overwhelmingly so, and she consciously resisted the natural urge to start writhing and moaning. And then the heat and throbbing in her pussy seemed to suddenly spread right out through her entire body to where it finally exploded in her head and she quietly panted as she accepted orgasm was taking her.

Magick Magazine No. 9

It was the day of the ritual and the first thing the girls noticed was that the horniness they experienced from ingesting the fertility potion hadn't subsided, despite the fact that they hadn't consumed any the previous night. In actuality, it seemed to have amplified to an immoral level. "My god, I think if I sat on my fist I would swallow it," Julia shamelessly commented, and Rainaa, despite her reservedness, full well understood what her friend was saying. "Do you think there really are eggs inside of us? My abdomen is bloated. ... So is yours."

"No, of course not," Rainaa assured her. We've just been eating too much island cuisine and downing too many cocktails. We are going to need to go on diets when we get back home."

As promised, festivities were abound. Everyone was clothed in a cheesecloth spawning veil, the girls' crossed over their breasts and then tied behind their necks resembling long dresses, and the hosts' just fastened around their waists. ... But nobody was permitted to wear underwear. Koa spent an hour weaving shells and seeds and flowers into Rainaa's long auburn tresses and then she helped him add some to his hair, too. Drums hammered in the background, providing atmosphere and the mouth-watering tropical seafood banquet was unending. And then night fell and they all watched as the full moon started to rise above the horizon.

Koa tickled the side of Rainaa's face and smiled, "Rainaa, would you like to come down into the water with me soon?"

It was all so romantic and she would probably have agreed even if her body wasn't burning with a desperate desire to copulate Koa's brains out. "Yes," she softly spoke.

But then, her small hand encompassed in his, when Koa began to walk her into the water, she froze.

What was she doing? She was about to walk into the ocean with someone - a stranger, who she assumed had drugged her with some jungle aphrodisiac. ...He was probably a member of some ritualistic sex cult. And had orgies... What the hell...?

Koa turned to her and smiled humbly before slowly and ever so gently reaching his other arm to rest at her side. "I'm nervous," she confessed in a low and shaky voice.

"I know..." he acknowledged comfortingly before leaning in and gently kissing her. Rainaa felt her lips tingle, and then she became aware of his other hand on her waist also. She felt his lips lift from hers, the cool ocean breeze quickly cooling their wetness, and she looked into his eyes – those amazingly opalescent eyes... And then very slowly, he started to walk backwards into the ocean, and Rainaa followed. Soon they were in as deep as two feet and Koa kneeled down onto the ocean floor, bringing Rainaa down with him, and then he reached up and lightly cupped the side of her face and started kissing her. Rainaa's eyes fluttered closed before she slowly raised her hands to his neck, gliding them beneath his beautiful long, sandy hair and she kissed him back.

His kiss was so sensual and his caress was making her body ache deliciously with desire. She could feel her breasts hungering for a touch and she pressed them into him. ...Her pussy too, quivering and desperately yearning for his attention. The air was subtly perfumed with Koa's pheromones and she was sure the aroma was getting thicker...

Rainaa gently opened her eyes – Koa's seeming to be somehow becoming even more luminous. Then she felt him gently cup his hands over her breasts and massage them through the very light fabric of the spawning veil, making her close her eyes again and purr with pleasure, before intensifying their kiss and probing his mouth deeply.

"May I lower this," Koa asked stroking the edge of the fabric on her chest.

"Yes..." she whispered. And then she sat on her feet, idle as her host reached up behind her neck and untied the cloth before ever so slowly lowering it to her waist. Koa then proceeded to softly tweak and tease her nipples, causing electricity to shoot through her body and fray at her pussy, striking her clit and her vagina simultaneously.

Rainaa moaned as she pulled him close, needing to feel his hard maleness compacting her breasts. She allowed one hand to meander down his back, exploring the contours of his muscular topography, the fever between her thighs ever heating, the butterflies in her stomach starting to flap their wings almost uncomfortably. She sighed audibly as she sucked on his bottom lip, kissing it, and then something in her stomach twinged almost painfully, making her suddenly jump and pull back, her eyes flying open and exhibiting concern. "Everything is okay, Rainaa," his calming voice informed her.

She looked up into his eyes, "I think I am starting to get cramps..."

"It's just your ova dropping down and pressing against your cervix. What you're feeling is the equivalent of labour pains," he explained.

"What? D-do I really have eggs inside of me?" she asked in a panic.

"Yes you do," he whispered breathily, somewhat turned on.

"Oh my god, what's happening to me? How do I get them out?" she screeched, her octaves ringing at a distressed level.

"Rainaa," he whispered huskily, "They will come out during the spawning..."

"I thought that was just a legend..."

"It is. But one that has endured the ages and still lives today..."

She searched his eyes for some kind of fraudulence but she could only see calm sincerity, and her voice quavering, she again asked, "Is it going to hurt?"

"Only the pain of a hundred very intense orgasms..." he offered as he pulled her back into him and kissed her hungrily once again.

Find our more about the mysterious merpeople of the Island of Salacia as DD Scarlet continues her Pagan tale with us next issue!

IMAGE CREDIT
http://www.mermanchristian.com
https://www.instagram.com/merman_chris

THE SOUTHERN & NORTHERN WITCH'S ALMANAC

JUNE - DECEMBER 2019

Sacred Days - Ancient Festivals - Commemorative Dates Moon Phases - Astronomical Alignments

All Collated In One Place For Your Easy Reference

by Shé D'Montford

Know when and why to work your magick by following Magick Magazine's almanac

All times are Australian Eastern Standard Time (AEST - UTC +10) - add 1 hour for Daylight Savings Time when applicable.

JUNE

01. 18:15 ♀ Venus 3°N of ○ Moon 04:33

03. 10:02 ● NEW MOON

04. 15:42 ☿ Mercury 4°N of ○ Moon

05. 15:05 ♂ Mars 1.6°N of ○ Moon

07. 23:21 ○ Moon at Perigee: 368,508 km 09:21

10. 05:59 ◑ FIRST QUARTER MOON

10.15 ♃ Jupiter at Opposition

16. 18:50 ♃ Jupiter 2°S of ○ Moon

17. 08:31 ○ FULL MOON

18. 18 ☿ Mercury 0.2° of ♂ Mars

19. 03:58 ♄ Saturn 0.5°N of ○ Moon

20. **The Day of Ceridwen.** Sacred to the Celtic Goddess of fertility. Traditionally celebrated in Ireland by tying a ribbon to a tree and making a wish.

Rural Dionysian - Lesser, or Rural, Dionysia, preserved ancient customs centered on a celebration of the first wine. This festival was timed to coincide with the "clearing of the wine," a final stage in the fermentation process occurring in the first cold snap after the Winter Solstice, when it was declared that Dionysus was reborn. Theatrical contest of singing and dancing were performed in his honor.

21. ☼ Sun Enters ♋ Cancer at the time of the solstice.

21. 15:54 Minor ❂ Sabbat. **YULE.** Winter Solstice Shortest day of the year. Winter Solstice can be between 21 - 23 June in the Southern hemisphere and the December 21- 23 in the northern Hemisphere. See notes on the Sabbats.

Wadjet, the Uracus Goddess, was regarded as governing the eleventh month of the Egyptian year.

CANCER - June 21- July 22

Cardinal sign of ▽ Water -

Planetary Ruler ○ Moon.

23. **St. John's Eve** – Northern Hemisphere – A Mid-summers magickal herb gathering night. Should be celebrated by us the night after Summer Solstice. A night for gathering and storing herbs as herb are at the height of their magickal properties on this night. See Sabbat notes about this night!

07:50 ○ Moon at Apogee: 404,549 km 17:50

23 ☿ Mercury at Greatest Elong: 25°E

24. **The festival of Fata**, the Roman Goddesses of fate and chance.

25. **Ganga Dashami** - Hindu

09:46 ◐ LAST QUARTER MOON

30. **Blodeuwedd's day** – Celtic celebration of beautiful women

JULY

02. 19:16 ● NEW MOON

19:23 ● Total Solar Eclipse; Sth America

04. 08:34 ☿ Mercury 3°S of ○ Moon

05. 04:54 ○ Moon at Perigee: 363,729 km 14:54

23 ☿ Mercury 4° of ♂ Mars

23 ⊕ Earth farthest from ☼ Sun (Aphelion 08:10 152,104,285km).

07. 07 ☿ Mercury at Aphelion

Nonae Caprotinae ("the nones of the wild fig"), the second festival of Juno, the chief Roman Goddess.

Tanabata or Star Festival (Japan)

Rhea / Cybil Festival Day also sacred to Dionysus

Anniversary of the Martyrdom of Bab (Baha'i)

09. 10:55 ◑ FIRST QUARTER MOON

16 ♄ Saturn at Opposition

Begins Celtic Tree Month of HOLLY- Gaelic: Tinne - July 9 - Aug 5

10. **Holda / Hel Day**- Norse Goddess of the underworld is honoured with black candles and rose petals on this day

11. **Theano Day**, wife of Pythagoras, "Theano shall contribute the greatness of her intellect"

13. 19:43 ♃ Jupiter 2°S of ○ Moon

15. **Isis - Osiris' Birthday**. A celebration of the Egyptian Mother Goddess of magick, power, beauty, and love and her twin brother/husband the Egyptian God of fertility, civilisation, agriculture, writing and the underworld, being borne on this day

The Rosalia - The Roman's feast of roses. The rose was especially sacred to Venus, as goddess of love.

Rosa Mundi - The Rose of the World, the Heart of Creation; the Consuming Fire. The Mother's festival, and is the time that we meditate most deeply upon our relationship to Her. She is the Maker and Shaper of each individual soul in its pure and perfect form. We are born from Her joy, and only in Her are we whole. At the Rosa Mundi rite for the handmaid, everyone is given a rose to hold during the contemplation. The Rose, the grandest, the noblest of Nature's symbols. To the Rosicrucian the Rose was the symbol of Nature, of the ever prolific and virgin Earth, considered as feminine and represented as a virgin woman by the Egyptian initiates, of Isis, the mother and nourisher of man. The altar is decked with roses and candles

Rath Yatra – Hindu

16. 07:27 ♄ Saturn 0.2°N of ○ Moon

21:31 ● Partial Lunar Eclipse;

21:38 ○ FULL MOON

19. **Great Panathenala Day One of Six Days** - Every year in the month of Phaophi, the second month of the floods, came the period of eleven days during which the capital celebrated the feast of Opet when Amun and his spouse Mut, the Karnak form of Isis, accompanied by the god Khonsu, proceeded ceremonially at the time of this 'divine emergence', giving the crowd a glimpse of the triad of its three great gods. The telltale number, eleven, points to the festival being the period of 'catching up' the lunar year to the solar by the intercalation of that many days to close the elevenday discrepancy between lunar and solar years. This would originally have been a festival to mark time before the rising of Sirius and the inauguration of the Egyptian New Year. The Nile began to rise at about the same time that the brilliant star Sirius, Sothis, 'the Dog Star', after having been invisible for a prolonged period, was first again observed in the sky

Athena's Day - the birthday of the goddess Athena, the daughter of Métis, the first wife of Zeus. The day of her birth was the day of the beginning of the ancient Greek new-year and was held every fifth year.

Aphrodite - the wedding of Adonis and Aphrodite... There was considerable variation in the date of the festival. In fifth century Athens they were held in April, in Ptolemaic Egypt in September, while under the Empire the accepted date was 19th July.

20. **Egyptian New Year** which is the birthday of Horus; or more accurately when The Dog Star, Sirius, rises in Leo between 6pm and midnight

21. 00:01 ○ Moon at Apogee: 405,480 km 10:01

Oghma's Day – Celtic Hercules –He carried a great club but did great deeds via the gift of the gab, and taught the Ogham alphabet to man.

Nana - the lioness, a form of Kybele, appears in the ancient art of India, Mesopotamia, and the Ancient Middle East from 3000 BC up to Classical times.

Damo - Daughter of Pythagoras and Theano. At his death, Pythagoras entrusted her with all the secrets of his philosophy, and gave her the unlimited care of his compositions.

22. ♌ **LEO** - July 23 – August 23

Fixed sign of △ Fire-

Planetary Ruler ☼ Sun

Neptunalia, the festival of Neptune, the Roman god of the sea.

24. **Last day of the Great Panathenala** or Egyptian new year festival.

Neith - A feast of lamps was also celebrated at Sais in Egypt in honor of Isis Neith. The ceremony took place in an under-chapel beneath the Temple. Lamps were carried in procession around the coffin of Osiris. 'In Sais the statue of Athena, whom they believe to be Isis, bore the inscription: I am all that has been and is and shall be, and none mortal hath lifted my Veil. In one of the Hermetic texts called "Peplos" (The Veil) it is said that the Veil "signified the Veil of the Universe, studded with stars, the manycoloured Veil of Nature, the famous Veil or Robe of Isis, that no mortal has raised". To raise the Veil of Isis means to see Nature as she really is, to understand what it is that underlies the manifestations of this world, and of the emotions which so move us, to see them in their ultimate reality, not veiled any longer... S(he) who is able to do that and so to face reality becomes consciously immortal.

25. 01:18 ☽ LAST QUARTER MOON
Salacia / Hygia- Goddess of salt & ▽ water, whose symbol was the pentagram; identified with the Greek Amphitrite, and regarded as the wife of Neptune. This festival is very old.
Hatshepsut the most famous of the female pharaohs, is honored for her magick and healing abilities on this day.
28. Delta- ♒ Aquarid Meteor Shower
Pythias - The mother of Pythagoras. He was named after her. She officiated at Delphi as the Pythian oracle.
29. **Guru Purnima / Asadha Purnima** - Hindu

AUGUST

01. 03:12 ● NEW MOON
02. 7:08 ○ Moon at Perigee: 359,398 km 17:08
Lughas' Day - Celtic – God of skill in crafts. A great hero that descends into the underworld to do battle with darkness, his brother on winter solstice (Yule). His body in the underworld was the Yule log. His victorious symbol is the decorated pine tree erected after his return on the 25th. Harvest Games, were held in honour of Lughas from Wales to Lyons.
Macha, Queen of Ireland - the Annual Fair of Macha held at Armagh was established to commemorate Queen Macha of the Golden Hair, who had founded the palace there. The Machas likewise were associated with this feast: The Three Machas are, according to Irish literary tradition, Macha wife of Nemed, Macha wife of Crurmchu and Macha the Red. The third Macha, of the Red, or Golden Hair reigned as Queen of Ireland c.377 BC.

✹ **Major Sabbat**: The Beginning of Spring – 2nd August or 15 degrees of ♌ Leo in the Southern Hemisphere, or February 2nd or 15 degrees of ♒ Aquarius in the Northern Hemisphere.
IMBOLC (im'molc or im'bolc) means, "in the belly of the mother," or Oimelc means "milk of ewes," for it is also Lambing Season, Candelmas, and Saint Briget's Day. The festival of lights in the southern Hemisphere- Northern Hemisphere Lughnasadh, the Celtic festival marking the harvest period. Also the festival of Lug, the Celtic hero god.
04. **Culhwch** – Celtic
06. **Begins Celtic Tree Month of HAZEL** - Gaelic: Coll - August 6 - September 2
07. 17:31 ☽ FIRST QUARTER MOON
09. 22:53 ♃ Jupiter 2°S of ○ Moon
23 ☿ Mercury at Greatest Elong: 19°W
The festival of Sol Invictus, the Roman all conquering Sun god.
Wiccan Festival of Fire Spirits. Good time to work with the △ fire element.
Chung Yuan - The Hungary Ghost Festival - (blend of Buddhist, Bon, Confucian and Taoist religions) **First** ○ **Full Moon In August** – This year it is a ♒ Aquarian full moon in August. The Chinese are still very partial to keeping the dead happy. They believe that ancestors can influence their joss (luck) in this life. This festival celebrates the time when spirits are let out of purgatory where they never get fed. At midnight, the ghosts must return to purgatory. You can acknowledge these lost souls by leaving bowls of noodles, sweetmeats, cakes and other treats in public places. I highly recommend going to the Chinese quarter of your capital city to enjoy this spectacular festival as lightening the burden of these lost souls can include performances of operas and puppet shows on street corners.
10. **Merlins day** - Celtic- today and on the 17th
11. **Puck Fair** a 3-day Irish feast that honours Robin Goodfellow, the famous mischievous sprite.
12. 10:05 ♄ Saturn 0°N of ○ Moon 20:05 Occn*
Peak Perseids Meteor shower, low in the north pre-dawn sky
13. 07 Perseid Meteor Shower
The Vertumnalia, the festival of Vertumnus, the Roman god of seasons, gardens, and orchards.
Festival of Hecate to be held after dark. The Greeks observed two days sacred to Hecate, one on the 13th of August and one on the 30th of November, whilst the Romans observed the 29th of every month as her sacred day. Hecate was originally a goddess of the wilderness and childbirth originating from Thrace, or among the Carians of Anatolia. Popular cults venerating her as a mother goddess integrated her persona into Greek culture as Ἑκατη. In Ptolemaic Alexandria, she became a goddess of sorcery (which means sister magick) and her role as the 'Queen of Ghosts.' Today she is often seen as a goddess of witchcraft.
14. 06 ♀ Venus Superior Conjunction
15. 12:29 ○ FULL MOON
Festival of Vesta the Goddess of Hearth Home and health celebrate her by lighting a sacred flame to her today.
Festival of Torches to Diana - Her chief festival. Her groves shone with a multitude of torches.
Funadama matsuri (Japanese) On August 15 at the Hodosan jinja, Saitama, the Funadama matsuri ("boat festival") is held. This festival dates from the Tokugawa period when travellers by raft from Chichibu to Eda prayed for safe passage on the Arakawa River.
Teej – Hindu - has become Indian Independence Day
17. 10:50 ○ Moon at Apogee: 406,244 km 20:50
Merlins day - Celtic- today and on the 10th
The Portunalia, the festival of Portunes, the Roman god of gates, doors, and harbours. At this festival, people would throw keys into the fire in order to bless them.
19. **The Vinalia**, the festival of Venus and Minerva, at that time temples and gardens were set apart for her, and then

The Standing Stone Circle at Glenn Innes
In the early morning mist at -12°c
Winter Solstice
Celtic Festival
NSW - Australia

Jayson Sharman PHOTOGRAPHY

the kitchen gardeners went on holiday. An old Vinalia invocation:- "I beseech Minerva and Venus, of whom the one protects the olive yard, and the other the garden and in her honour the rustic Vinalia has been established."
Raksha Bandhan- Humanity Day- (Hindu)
20. **The Festival Of Consus**, the Roman god of good council.
23. 14:56 ☽ LAST QUARTER MOON
The Volcanalia, the festival of Vulcan, the Roman god of fire. This took place during the height of the Mediterranean drought and the period of highest risk of fire. On the banks of the river Tiber, fires were lighted on which living fish were sacrificed.
Genia (Genie, Genius – Higher Self) of Personal Fate. The threads of Moira draw all things in life together. Her particular symbols are the wheel and the scales. This day is especially one for examining the direction of one's soul and making resolutions for the future.
Nemesia - in memory of deceased persons. The Goddess Nemesis was supposed to defend the relics and memory of the dead from all insult.

♍ **VIRGO** 24 Aug – 23 Sept
Mutable sign of ▽ Earth -
Planetary Ruler ☿ Mercury.

25. **Ops** - Abundance. Consivia was the old Italian Goddess of fertility, sowing and reaping. Only the Vestals and one of the pontifices could attend. Her abode was in the earth, so her worshipers invoked her while seated and touching the ground.
Onam – Hindu.
26. **Luonnotar** – A Finnish Goddess, or the Water Mother, was the Creatrix of the World. Upon her knees the duck laid the six golden and the one iron egg from which the world was made.
28. **Raksha-Bandhan-** Hindu
30. 10:37 ● NEW MOON
15:57 ☉ Moon at Perigee: 357,177 km 01:57
31. **Hathor** – Her birthday, Thoth 1, was the beginning of the New Year on the fixed Alexandrian Calendar. Before dawn the priestesses would bring Hathor's image out onto the terrace to expose it to the rays of the rising sun, followed by ladies cracking mystic whips, crowned with flowers and leading a drunken carnival.

SEPTEMBER

02. 10 ♂ Mars Conjunction with ☉ Sun
Father's Day.
03. **Viking 2 Mars Landing** 1976.
The Celtic Tree Calendar Month VINE Gaelic: Muinn - September 3 - September 30
The Vine is the symbol of creeping sensuality and entangling emotions. A hardy, long-lived plant. It's symbol, the white swan represents the white ghosts or the white phantom, Gwenhwyvar. The equinox is a time when for a brief moment all is in balance. The light and the dark hold equal positions, the balance of the mundane and the supernatural; the mortal and the immortal. This Ogham represents the letter M in the Tree Alphabet as well as Muinn in the Calendar. Vine is "The whispered words of sweet poetry."
04. **The Celtic Feast of Rhiannon**
Krishna Janmashtami Krishna took birth at midnight on the ashtami or the 8th day of the Krishnapaksha or dark fortnight in the Hindu month of Shravan (August-September). This auspicious day is called **Janmashthami.** - Hindu.
Geronimo Surrendered 1886.
05. **Shikshak Divas.**
Teacher's Day.
06. 03:10 ☽ FIRST QUARTER MOON
06:52 ♃ Jupiter 2°S of ☉ Moon
07. **National Threatened Species Day.**
Healer's Day - Wiccan – A day to honour all forms of healers and to do a ritual requesting healing.
The Greek Feast of Asclepigenaia - An Eleusinian Priestess.
Mao Tse-Tung died 1976
08. 13:53 ♄ Saturn 0°N of ☉ Moon 23:53 Occn*
11. **The Matriarchy of Egypt**
All Queens were High Priestesses of Egypt, and Initiates of the Inner Mysteries. Their power was hidden, but it was they who ruled Egypt through the Pharoah of the time, whether he was their brother, husband or father. No man could become Pharoah (the Living Horus, the resurrected Osiris) other than by marriage to such a Lady of the Royal Line which ran through the female side, and derived ultimately from Isis.
Padmasambhava Day –Tibetan Buddhist.
Ethiopian New Year's Day – Rastafarian.
12. **Hildegard of Bingen** (1098-1179) – One of the first campaigners of women's rights against the Catholic Church from within the Celtic Church in Germany. She wrote over a hundred letters on this subject to emperors, popes, bishops, archbishops, nuns and the nobility, as well as seventy poems and nine books describing her visions of the universe, dictated to her secretary, Monk Volmar. In her own words, "When 1 was forty-two years and seven months old, a burning light of tremendous brightness coming from heaven poured into my entire mind. Like a flame that does not burn but enkindles, it inflamed my entire heart and my entire breast, just like the sun that warms an object with its rays... All of a sudden, I was able to taste of the understanding of the narration of books. ....". In a letter to Abbot Adam of Ebrach, Hildegard reported seeing in a vision "an extraordinarily beautiful Young Woman wearing shoes which seemed of purest gold whom the whole creation called- Lady". The image spoke to a female human of sapphire blue and said: "Dominion is yours on the day of your power in the radiance of the saints. I have brought you forth from my own womb before the daystar. (♀ Venus)" Then Hildegard heard a voice tell her, "The young woman whom you see is Love. She has her tent in Eternity... For it was Love which was the source of this creation in the beginning…". Hildegard asked, "Why does the whole Creation call this maiden "Lady?" She received the reply: "Because it was from Her that all creation proceeded, since Love as the First. She made everything".In Hildegard's writing and her illuminations one can see influences of the ancient Goddess religions, of the Roman Aurora, The Egyptian Isis, the old Germanic Horsel, and the Hebrew Hokma.
13. 13:32 ☉ Moon at Apogee: 406,378 km
Ramadan Begins Muslim.
Egyptian Day Of The Dead – On this day ancient Egyptians lit fires to honour the dead and the Goddess Nephthys.
Rosh Hashanah/Jewish New Year -13-14 September.
14. 04:33 ☉ FULL MOON
15. **Ganesh/Vinayak Chaturthi**
Ganesha — the festival to celebrate and glorify the elephant-deity riding a mouse. A clay model of Lord Ganesha is made 2-3 months prior to the day of Ganesh Chaturthi. On the day of the festival, it is placed on raised platforms in homes. The priest invokes life into the idol.
17. **Astraea / Dike / Virgo**
The Greeks call Virgo Dike or Justitia), because she is thought to hold the neighboring Scales (♎Libra).
It is fabled that The Starry Goddess, Astraea, returned in the iron age as the impersonation of Justice, whose symbol was the Scales, to praise equity. "She dwelt on earth and met men face to face, nor ever disdained in olden time the tribes of men and women, but mingling with them took her seat, immortal though she was. Her, men called Justice (Dike)... Nor yet in that age had men knowledge of hateful strife... Even so long as the earth nurtured the Golden Age, she had her dwelling on earth... Yet in that Silver Age was she still upon the earth, but from the echoing hills at eventide she came alone. But when they, too, were dead, and when, more ruinous than they which went before, the Race of Bronze was born, who were the first to forge the sword of the highwayman, and the first to eat the flesh of the ploughing-ox, then verily did Justice loathe that race of men and fly heavenward and took up that abode, where even now in the night-time the Maiden (Virgo) is seen…". (Aratus, Phaenomena) Upholder of Justice: Trump VIII of Tarot.
Maat - Goddess who protects Truth with her outstretched wings. She sits on the fulcrum of the scales that balance the deeds of the heart against her one white feather.
18. **Luang Phor Sodh attained Dhammakaya** (lunar) Thai Buddhist.
19. **The Fast of Thoth**, this day long fast honors the Egyptian god of wisdom and magic.
Lailat - Ul - Bara'h - The Night of Forgiveness- Muslim.
City Dionysia – were the main festivities for the God Dionysus, as well as being an urban carnival or Komos. They were held around the time of the Spring Equinox, about three months after the Rural Dionysia, to celebrate the end of winter and the arrival of the new vine-growing season. It was celebrated with a great drama festival. Dionysus was also the god of acting, music, and poetic inspiration. Tragedy plays were more important than comedy at this festival. The prize for the winner of the tragedy festival was a goat, (the Greek word for goat is the origin of the word "tragedy") a common symbol of Dionysus, and his tragic early life.
20. **Luang Phor** Sodh attained Dhammakaya (solar) Thai Buddhist
22. 02:41 ☽ LAST QUARTER MOON
23. 07:50 ☼ Sun on Equator (Equinox 17:50)
28. 02:27 ☉ Moon at Perigee: 357,803 km 12:27
28. 18:26 ● NEW MOON
29. 04:15 ☿ Mercury 7°S of ☉ Moon
30 Sept **Greater Eleusinian Mysteries** – Day Eight of Nine Days
On the eighth day the Lesser Mysteries were repeated.

OCTOBER

1. **Greater Eleusinian Mysteries** – Day Nine of Nine Days
The last day of the Great Mysteries at Eleusis was devoted to plenty in its liquid form. This was the day of the plemochoai, 'the pourings of plenty'. So called, also, were the two unstable circular vases that were set up for this ceremony... The plemochoai were poured into a cleft in the earth... one vessel was set up in the east, and the other on the west side, and both overturned. The liquid with which they had been filled is not named. (Kerenyi, Eleusis.)
The Celtic Tree Calendar Month IVY - Gaelic: Gort - October 1 - October 28
In contrast to the Vine, Ivy is evergreen, and it represents the immortal spirit. The Celts associate Ivy with their lunar goddess Arianrhod and their ritual to her marked the opening of the portal to the fairy worlds through the dark side of the moon. The Butterfly is their symbol. Ivy represents mysterious and the mystical spiritual worlds. This Ogham represents the letter G in the Tree Alphabet as well as Gort in the Calendar. The Ivy is "The Wild Boar of ruthless hunt."
The Festival Of Fides, the Roman Goddess of good faith, honesty, and oaths.
Guiding Spirits Day – Wiccan festival to guardian and guiding spirits celebrated by light a candle on the altar or a blazing fir in the home fireplace.
2. **Gandhi Jayanti.** Birthday of Mahatma Gandhi (1869 - 1948), India's "Father of the Nation".
3. 20:23 ♃ Jupiter 2°S of ☉ Moon
The Festival Of Dionysus, the Greek god of wine and revelry, also known as Bacchus to the Romans.
4. **Celtic Feast day of Pwyll.** Pwyll, the Celtic ruler of the Otherworld, was given 'The Stone,' one of four treasures given to him for safekeeping. The Stone represents the right of the Kings and Queens to have divine power.

5. 16:47 ◐ FIRST QUARTER MOON

20:48 ♄ Saturn 0.3°N of ☉ Moon

6. **Daylight Savings Starts-** Australia
7. **World Animal Day**
9. **The Festival Of Felicitas**, the Roman Goddess of good luck and joy.
10. 18:29 ○ Moon at Apogee: 405,902 km 04:29

Birthday of Luang Phor Sodh (solar) – Thai Buddhist

11. **Pitr-Paksha ends / Mahalaya** is an auspicious occasion observed seven days before the Durga Puja, and heralds the advent of Durga, the goddess of supreme power. It is an invocation or invitation to the mother goddess to descend on earth - "Jago Tumi Jago."

Thanksgiving Day (Canada)

The Meditrinalia, the festival of Meditrina, the Roman Goddess of healing, wine, and health.

12. **Navaratri** begins. Literally the nine nights invokes the energy aspect of the universal mother, commonly referred to as "Durga," which literally means the remover of miseries of life. She is also referred to as "Devi" (goddess) or "Shakti" (energy or power). God is motionless, absolutely changeless, and the Divine Mother Durga, does everything.

Birthday of Alistair Crowley- on this day in 1875.

The Festival Of Fortuna Redux, the Roman Goddess of successful journeys and safe returns from those journeys.

Our Lady of Fatima. The last appearance of the Virgin Mary at Fatima took place on 13 October 1917. The Greater Eleusinian Mystery was, 1 believe, manifested at Fatima. Here we have people seeing a Golden Disc bringing from the sky the apparition of a woman robed in white. The visions were shown to three children, and occurred on each thirteenth of the month, from May to October; so including the ancient dates of the Mysteries of the Goddesses. At the culmination in October, seventy thousand onlookers saw a sun disc revolve and show spectroscopic change; they called it 'the dancing sun'. (Olivia Robertson, The Call of Isis, p125) 'It is already time that each one of us accomplishes holy deeds of his own initiative and reforms his own life...''

Eid Al Fitr End Of Ramadan - Muslim

13. 21:08 ○ FULL MOON

The Festival Of Fontus, the Roman god of springs.

15. **St Teresa of Avila** Saint of the Ecstatic Orgasm – Born October 15 1515 and died October 15 1582.

Pandrosus- The first priestess of Athena.

18. **Durga Puja (Maha Saptami)** Twice a year, close to our major Sabbats of the at the cross quarters, Hindus observe nine days of ceremonies, rituals, fasts and feasts in honour of the supreme mother goddess Durga and her aspects of Lakshmi and Saraswati – 3 days for each. 6 days after the commencements is Durga's big day!

End of Buddhist Lent – Thai Buddhist

Drawing Down the Sun – Gardinerian Wicca – The priest of a coven perform a ceremony in honour of the horned god of fertility and wild animals

19. **Dhak Bad Tewo Devorohana**, at 9:00 a.m. "Coming down from the deva world", a special alms round circling the main temple building, in memory of the return of the Buddha from Tavatimsa or second heaven, after proclaiming the Dhamma to his mother in order to repay her kindness. Thai Buddhist

The Armilustrium, the second festival of Mars, the Roman god of war. On this day, military arms were ritually purified and put in storage for winter.

20. 04:00 ☿ Mercury at Greatest Elong: 25°E

Navaratri ends

Birthday of the Bab -Baha'i

21. 12:39 ◑ LAST QUARTER MOON

23:00 Orionid Meteor Shower

Selket- The Egyptian sky-diagram, first found on a coffin-fragment excavated in Asyut of about 2050 BC shows above the Lion a Scorpio Goddess, identifiable with the Babylonian goddess Ishhara. Selket heralded the sunrise through her temples at the autumn equinox about 3700-3500 BC and was the symbol of Isis in the pyramid ceremonials.

Ishhara- Scorpio was known to the Babylonians as the female scorpion Ishhara, the wife of the Archer.

Demeter- The month for sowing, in the season of the Plciades, the Egyptians call Athyr (sacred to Hathor), the Athenians Pyanepsion and the Bcoeotians Damatrios, 'the month sacred to Demeter'.

The Celtic Feast Day of Cerridwen

Vijaya Dashami/ Dusshera or Vijayadashami- This occurs on the "tenth" day following the Navratri. It is a festival to celebrate the triumph of good over evil, and marks the defeat and death of the demon king Ravana in the epic Ramayana. Huge effigies of Ravana are burnt amidst the bangs and booms of firecrackers.

22. **Labour Day** NZ

♏ SCORPIO Oct 24 – Nov 22

Fixed Sign of ▽ Water-

Planetary Ruler ♇ Pluto

---

24 October |Sun enters *Scorpio@ 5.15am *She*'- is this right?*

Birthday of Luang Phor Sodh (lunar) Thai Buddhist.

United Nations Day

Spirits of the Air Day – Wiccan day of incense offering to the air elementals.

25. **Lakshmi Puja / Sharad Purnima-** On the full moon night following Dusshera or Durga Puja, Hindus worship Lakshmi ceremonially at home, pray for her blessings, and invite neighbours to attend the Puja. It is believed that on this full moon night the goddess herself visits the homes and blesses the inhabitants with wealth. A special worship is also offered to Lakshmi on the auspicious Diwali night

26. 10:41 ○ Moon at Perigee: 361,316 km 20:41

28. 03:38 ● NEW MOON

29. 13:34 ♀ Venus 4°S of ☉ Moon

The Celtic Tree Calendar Month of REED - Gaelic: Ngetal - Oct29 – Nov25- Identified with what is submerged or hidden, the reed represents the mysteries of death. The Fire Feast of Samhain this month celebrates the dead and the boundary between the worlds thinning, thus it represents the hidden roots to all life. The Reed is associated with a saviour and a custodian. The Reed is also the symbol of Royalty. The White Hounds represent the dogs that guard the lunar mysteries. There is no translation or letter usage of Ngetal in the Celtic Tree Alphabet. Reed is "The restless noise of the wine dark sea"

Karwa Chauth: Fast for Married Women- A ritual of fasting observed by married Hindu women seeking the longevity, well-being, and prosperity of their husbands. All wives expect lavish gifts from their husbands! Unmarried women, widows, and spinsters are barred from observing this fast. No food or water can be taken after sunrise. Shiva, Parvati and their son Kartikeya are worshipped on this day along with the 10 'karwas' (earthen pots) filled with sweets. The Karwas are given to daughters, sisters and female friends along with gifts. At night when the moon appears, women break their fast after offering water to the moon. In the evening, the fasted women party, feast, and dress up in special clothes, usually a red or pink sari, jewellery, with 'mehendi' or henna patterns on the hands and decorative 'bindis' on the forehead. The fasted women from all over the neighbourhood gather in a group and narrate mythological stories that underscore the significance of Karwa Chauth. This festival comes 9 days before Diwali on 'kartik ki chauth', i.e., on the fourth day of the new moon immediately after Dusshera, in the month of 'Karthik' (October-November). 'Chauth' means the 'fourth day' and 'Karwa' is an earthen pot with a spout - a symbol of peace and prosperity - that is necessary for the rituals.

31. 04 ☿ Mercury 2° of ♀ Venus

14:22 ♃ Jupiter 1°S of ☉ Moon

Kathin - During the month following Ok Phansa, between the full moons of October and November. New robes will be offered to the monks on that day. – Thai Buddhist

Lailat- Ul- Qadr- The Night of Power- Muslim

Beltane Major |Solar Sabbat 31st Oct to 1st Nov is when **Beltane** is celebrated in the southern hemisphere see "This Season Sabbats" for more Beltane details. – **Samhain Eve -** Northern Hemisphere – **Day One of Three Days**

The Goddess Samhain- The Goddess of the first day of winter. Several Irish authors derive the name Samhain from the Semitic word Shamiyim, or with the Phoenician Samen, meaning "Heaven." "Red Hanrahan on Samhain Night came to the point where he could walk no longer, so sat down on the heather where he was, in the heart of Slieve Echtge. And after a while he took notice that there was a door close to him, and a light coming from it, and he wondered that being so close to him he had not seen it before. And he rose up and, tired as he was, went in at the door, and although it was night-time outside, it was daylight he found within. And presently he met with an old man that had been gathering summer thyme and yellow flagflowers, and it seemed as if all the sweet smells of summer were with him. And with that he brought him into a very big shining house, and every grand thing that Hanrahan had ever heard of, and every colour he had ever seen, was in it. There was a high place at the end of the house, and on it there was sitting in a high chair a woman, the most beautiful the world ever saw, having a blond pale face and flowers about it, but she had the tired look of one that had been long waiting. And there were sitting on the step below her chair four grey old women, and the one of them was holding a great cauldron in her lap; and another a great stone upon her knees, and heavy as it was it seemed light to her; and another of them had a very long spear that was made of pointed wood; and the last of them had a sword that was without a scabbard. Then the first of the old women rose up, holding the cauldron between her two hands, and she said, 'Pleasure'; then the second old woman rose up with the stone in her arms and she said, Tower'; and the third old woman rose up with a spear in her hand, and she said, 'Courage'; and the last of the old women rose up having the sword in her hands, and she said, 'Knowledge'. And then the four old women went out of the door bringing their four treasures with them. (Yeats, Mythologies, p220.) All-Hallows, is the feast of the dead in Pagan and Christian times, signalising the close of harvest and the initiation of the winter season, lasting until May. Hallowe'en was perhaps of old the most important feast, since the Celts would seem to have dated the beginning of the year from it rather than Beltane. In ancient Ireland, a new fire used to be kindled every year on Hallowe'en on the Eve of Samhain, and from this sacred flame all the fires in Ireland were kindled. Such a custom points strongly to Samhain (the first of November) as New Year's Day. The fairies (the sidhe pronounced the shay) were imagined as particularly active at this season, from which the half-year is reckoned. The Ultonians held of the fair of Samhain in the plain of Murthemne (County Louth) every year: and nothing whatever was done by them during that time but games and races, pleasure and amusement, and feasting: and it is from this circumstance that the Trenae Samna (three days of Sarnhain) are still observed throughout Ireland. All Celtic feasts begin in the evening at sundown about 6pm which was the start of the next day (Not midnight)... its activities still mark Hallowe'en as one of the great 'spirit nights' of the Celtic peoples. On this evening the living reached out to the souls of the dead whilst the veil between the worlds was the thinnest. Families sat up till midnight and little cakes, known as Soul Cakes, were eaten by everyone. There were still a few children in 1938, going from door to door 'souling' for cakes or money by singing a song. As the clock struck twelve there was silence, for at this hour the souls of the dead would revisit their earthly homes. There were candles burning in every room to guide them. and there was a glass of wine on the table to refresh them.

Tlachtga- also had a feast dedicated to her. The Fire Festivals are distinctly Female in nature. Samhain is the festival of Hecate, the Old Moon Goddess. The eight local mother goddesses of Ireland were then the patrons of the great seasonal feasts and assemblies. King Tuathal Teachtrnhar in the year 79 built the royal scat of Tlachtga, where the fire Tlachtga was ordained to be kindled. The use of this sacred fire was to summon the priests, augurs and druids of Ireland to repair thither and assemble upon the eve of All Saints. No other fire should be kindled upon that night throughout the kingdom, so that the fire that was to be used in the country was to be derived from this holy fire.

The Isia – Day One of Four Days- Isis, like Demeter, had two great festivals, one in the spring and another in the autumn. The autumnal celebration consisted of a passion play which continued for four days – although the date varied in different places, it usually began on October 31st and ended on November 3rd. Actors impersonating Isis, Nephthys, Anubis, Horus, searched for the body of Osiris. They shrouded the gilded image of a cow with a black linen as a sign of the Goddess in mourning, they lead the black-veiled golden cow seven times round the temple of Helios and this perambulation is called the seeking for Osiris.' Unlike The Elusian mysteries it was not conducted in strict secrecy, for it was a public out doors performance and pageant of the resurrection of Osiris by Isis. "Come to thy house, O fair youth, that thou mayest see me. I am thy sister, whom thou lovest; thou shalt not part from me. Yet, doth my heart yearn after thee and mine eyes desire thee. Come to her who loves thee, Come to thy sister, come to thy Wife, thou shalt not be far from me. I call after thee and weep my brother, my brother." (A Lament of Isis from the play.) The most stirring and most suggestive, incorporating a sex act, was the commemoration of the Finding of Osiris and the reassembling him. The 14th part his penis was missing so Isis made an artificial one, had sex with it and conceived Horus. This festival was held at Abydos and at Rome at the beginning of each November.

Bau/Gula
In the old days of Gudea of Lagash the year commenced with the festival of the Goddess Bau in the middle of October; in the later Babylon of Hammurabi the feast was transferred to the spring, and the first month of the year began in March. However, the older calendar of Babylonia had been already carried to the West. The ancient Canaanite year began in the autumn in what the later calendar reckoned the seventh month. The festal calendar of Lagash going back to Sumerian times is well known. There the New Year Festival was celebrated with the marriage of the goddess Bau to the god Ningirsu.

Gwydion the Dagda
The day of his awakening and magickal empowerment
Rebirth of Caileach Beara, the Celtic Goddess who turned to stone on May 1 (Beltane).

NOVEMBER
1. **Beltane -** |Major Sabbat – See the article "This seasons Sabbats."
Day of the Dead in most South American and Mexican cultures. Offerings of food and strong drink are offered to the spirits of the deceased.
Divali –Sikh
Isia – Day Two of Four Days
Samhain – Day Two of Three Days
Tea- The Assembly of Tara, the ancient religious and political centre of Ireland, was under the patronage of the goddess Tea, and took place on Samhain. Today this ancient site is being destroyed to make way for a freeway. There is a tradition in early Irish legends of holding the sacred feast of Samhain on the shores of lakes. In the story of 'The Dream of Angus', the feast is held by the side of Loch Bel Dracon by swan-girls, symbolic of otherworldly souls, wearing magic necklets.
All Saints- The Christian Churchs celebrates the presence of All Saints and All Souls following the vigil of All Souls' Eve by tending and tiding the grave plots in the local cemetery.
Celtic Feast Day if - Lly
2. 07:31   ♄ Saturn 0.5°N of ☉ Moon
Isia - Day Three of Four Days
Samhain – Day Three of Three Days- On the third day of the Seeking of Osiris the celebrants 'go down to the sea at night-time; and the keepers of the robes and the priests bring forth the hallowed chest containing a small golden coffer, into which they pour some drinkable water which they have taken up, and a great shout arises from the company for joy that Osiris is found. Then they knead some fertile soil with the water and mix in spices and incense of a very costly sort, and fashion there from a crescent-shaped figure which they clothe and adorn.' (Plutarch, De Iside et Osiride)
All Souls' Day- The feast of All Saints on November 1st was instituted in the ninth century, and the feast of All Souls' Day on November 2nd in 998 AD
Anniversary of the **Crowning of Haile Selassie** -Rastafarian

Dance of the Fiery Stars - a Dionysus ritual
3. **Gaelic New Year's Day**
Isia – Day Four of Four Days (The Hilaria)- Then Isis fanned the cold clay with her wings, breathed her own life into the nostrils of Osiris and with the help of spells from Thoth accomplished the resurrection of Osiris to a second and eternal life. As he lay there reconstituted, she fluttered over his erect phallus in the form of a white kite and conceived the golden falcon, Horus, who was to avenge the death of his father. This day was marked in the Roman calendar with the name Hilaria, because the crowd shouted for joy, 'Osiris has been found!' The celebrants were given over to the most unrestrained rejoicing, since the God, now risen to immortality, would assess all who had become divine by drinking the milk of Isis.
4. 10:23   ☾ FIRST QUARTER MOON
6. 00:00 ♉ Taurid Meteor Shower
Melbourne Cup Day
7. 08:37   ☉ Moon at Apogee: 405,060 km 18:37
9. **Diwali — the Festival of Lights! Day One**
Durga Puja - Kali Puja in Bengal
Is a four-day celebration that is the biggest of all Hindu festivals as the celebration of life, its enjoyment and goodness. Every household cleans their houses and lights up candles all over their houses. Children and adults set off firecrackers all night. No one sleeps on first that night. Durga/Kali is honoured as representing feminine strength, motherly love and dynamic energy that mocks human ignorance. Mythology says that Shiva and Kali are the originating couple of the universe but Kali even mocks Shiva, as if she herself is the unique source of everything. In reflection during this celebration, all women are honoured as mothers and sisters and given sweets. Begin and end this celebration by ritually cleansing your self and your home. Light a candle, sit quietly, shut your eyes, withdraw the senses, concentrate on this supreme light that illuminates the soul. Originally a harvest festival it is linked the worship of Mother Kali, the celebration of the marriage of Lakshmi with Lord Vishnu, Ganesha, and commemorates the return of Lord Rama along with Sita and Lakshman from his fourteen year long exile and vanquishing the demon-king Ravana. In Jainism, it is the great event of Lord Mahavira attaining the eternal bliss of nirvana. All celebrated with lights and firecrackers on each night. It is believed that on this day, Goddess Parvati played dice with her husband Lord Shiva, and she decreed that whosoever gambled on Diwali night would prosper the ensuing year. The first day of the festival Naraka Chaturdasi marks the vanquishing of the demon Naraka by Lord Krishna and his wife Satyabhama.
10. **Celtic Feast day of – Arawen**
Diwali — the Festival of Lights! Day Two - Amavasya,
The second day of Deepawali, marks the worship of Lakshmi, the Goddess of wealth, in her most benevolent mood, fulfilling the wishes of her devotees.
Reason- On November 10th 1793 a festival was held in Notre Dame de Paris in honour of 'Reason and Liberty,' represented by women. Mlle Candeille wore a red Phrygian cap, a white frock, a blue mantle, and tricolour ribbons. Her head was filleted with oak-leaves **The Festival Of Fontus**, the Roman god of springs.. In the cathedral a sort of 'Temple of Philosophy' was erected on a mound, and in this temple Mlle Candeille was installed. Young girls crowned with oak-leaves were her attendants, and sang hymns in her honour.
Kali Puja- Special rituals to Kali on the 2nd day of the Diwali
11. **Diwali — the Festival of Lights! Day Three - Kartika Shudda Padyami**
The third day of Deepawali that Bali steps out of hell and rules the earth according to the boon given by Lord Vishnu, who in his dwarf incarnation vanquished the tyrant Bali, and banished him to hell. Bali was allowed to return to earth once a year, to light millions of lamps to dispel the darkness and ignorance, and spread the radiance of love and wisdom. On the 3rd day a white-buffalo is offered to the Goddess, so you may leave her a small offering of bull or buffalo meat before her image on your personal altar
12. 13:34 ○ FULL MOON
23:00 ♉ Taurid Meteor Shower
Diwali — the Festival of Lights! Day Four - Yama Dvitiya /Bhai Dooj
On the fourth day of Deepawali, sisters invite their brothers to their homes, ritualise their love by putting an auspicious tilak or a vermilion mark on the forehead of their brothers, and perform an aarti of him by showing him the light of the holy flame as a mark of love and protection from evil forces. Sisters are lavished with gifts, goodies, and blessings from their brothers.
Ascension of 'Abdu'l-Bahá - Baha'i - **Anniversary of the Birth of Baha'u'llah -** Baha'i -
16. **Sangha Day** – Buddhist –
18. 05:00 ♌ Leonid Meteor Shower
19. 21:11 ☽ LAST QUARTER MOON
22. **St Cecilia -** A Roman lady of the third century, patroness of music, and of the blind.
Thanksgiving – Interfaith

♐ **SAGITTARIUS-** Nov 23 – Dec 22
Mutable Sign of △ Fire -
Planetary Ruler ♃ Jupiter

23. 07:54 ○ Moon at Perigee: 366,721 km 17:54
Artemis/Diana- The Romans assigned the virgin Goddess of hunting and the moon, Diana, to Sagittarius. The month of Sagittarius is a sacred time to the Goddesses of Menstruation.
Ishtar
In Babylon, the Sabbatu of the moon-goddess was at the full moon, and it was then that she was thought to be menstruating. Women who live

closely together will often come to menstruate simultaneously. That is why menstruation has often been called The Wise Wound. It is therefore possible that her colleges of priestesses menstruated in synchrony with each other and in sympathy with the Moon. The Sabbaths of the Jews were closely related in their origin to the Babylonian Sabbaths, but it is strange to us to think that the prohibitions connected with 'Sabbath observance' are, in their far-off origins, menstrual taboos connected with the belief that the moon is herself a woman having a monthly period. 'Menstruation' literally means 'moon-change.' In Babylon, the two most important points of the Moon's course, from the religious point of view, were the full moon (shabattum), and the day of the moon's total disappearance (bubbulum). The latter was marked by fasting, prayers, and other rites.

Hathor
The goddess Hathor, the Venus of the Egyptians presided over the Western quarter of Thebes. It was into her arms that the sun sinking behind the mountain, was poetically supposed to be received, and in this character answered also to Night.

Al,Uzzah
'The Great One', the Arabian Venus lies behind the Muslim holy day, which is Friday, always considered a lucky day for marriage. The colours of Muslim flags unconsciously honour the female element in displaying the green, or the vert, or the woman's colour, or Friday colour, that of the Muslim Sabbath. This green is that of the Venus of Mecca.

Freya
Freya was esteemed the mother of all the gods. She was worshipped as the goddess of love and pleasure, who bestowed on her votaries a variety of delights, particularly happy marriage, and easy childbirths. To Freya the sixth day of the week was consecrated, which still bears her name, Friday.

Shekinah
Shekinah, the magickal light over the ark of the covenant was thought to embody the form of a divine queen and bride, who joined them every Friday at dusk to bring them joy and happiness on the Sacred Sabbath meal. According to Raphael Patai **'Sabbath'** is the name of the Goddess who is the consort of the Jewish God. Just as in Tantric Hinduism, so Jehovah had his lover, Sabbath. Often confused with Shekinah who, to this day, in every Jewish temple or synagogue she is welcomed in the Friday evening prayers with the words, 'Come, O bride! Friday night, the Eve of the Sabbath, is the time when man comes together with his wife and the Shekinah fills the house. The Sabbath itself, Saturday, is kept holy and no masculine business venture or work is undertaken, in the Goddess's holy afterglow of loving intercourse between man and woman. Torah scholars perform marital intercourse precisely on Friday night for the reason that the earthly union was symbolic of the heavenly marriage between Jehovah and his Bride, Sabbath or Sacred Seventh, which generates Shekinah. The Hebrew tribes who originally worshipped Ashera, Ashteroth and Astart-Anath by pouring out libations to the Queen of Heaven as the modern Jews do every Friday.

The Virgin Mary
She is called by orthodox Catholic Fathers, The Moon of the Church, Our Moon, Spiritual Moon, The Perfect and Eternal Moon...

Manat/Allaat
Manat was the Arabian Goddess of the Moon, and when combined with the powers of Venus was known as Allaat – spelt in exactly the same way as the present Arabic word for God, Allaah. The Goddess is implicitly the foundation of Islam, whether present-day Arabs will confirm or deny it.

Mene/Selene
Dianna 2 other faces in ancient Greek myth.

Prosymne
Another face of Demeter in her underworld aspect, as the new moon

Hecate
Hecate, the new or dark moon, is generally taken to be the same as ta blending of Dianna the Moon and Proserpine. Hence her classical epithets Triceps and Triformis; referring to her other three faces and the three phases of the Selene first quarter Dianna Full and Mene last quarter. Eggs and onions, used to purify the house on the 30th of each month, were deposited for Hecate at three cross-roads. In the Julian calendar the old divisions of the lunar month were also retained... These were (a) the Kalendae, marking the first appearance of the new moon; (b) the Nonae, marking the first quarter; (c) the Idus, marking the full moon.

Govardhan Puja / Kali Puja

24. 09:02 ♂ Mars 4°S of ○ Moon

Guru Nanak Jayanti

25. 02:50 ☿ Mercury 2°S of ○ Moon

Esbat ○ Full Moon @ 12.30am in #Gemini

St Catherine
A Christian version of Nemesis, Goddess of the Wheel of Fate from which we get the custom of Catherin wheels. Burning wheels rolled down hills in the pagan fire festivals.

26. 15:06 ● NEW MOON

Day of Covenant – Baha'i

28. 10:00 ☿ Mercury at Greatest Elong: 20°W

28. 10:49 ♃ Jupiter 0.5°S of ○ Moon: Occn.

28. 18:50 ♀ Venus 2°S of ○ Moon

29. 21:12 ♄ Saturn 1°N of ○ Moon

DECEMBER

1. **The Festival Of Poseidon**, the Greek god of the sea. Poseidon is also the god of rebirth

Crowley's "Greater Feast" A celebration to commemorate the death of Aleister Crowley on this day in 1947 *e.v.*

4. 06:58 ◑ FIRST QUARTER MOON

The Festival Of Bona Dea, Women Only Day - Roman fertility Goddess with secret rites in the house of prominent Roman magistrates. all representations of men and beasts were removed.

5. 04:09 ○ Moon at Apogee: 404,447 km 14:09

Faunalia (Roman) The festival of Faunus, the Roman god of wild nature and fertility. (A "Blokes World" day) Masculine balance of the above.

6 Earliest | Sunrise for the year – What would you like to start anew? Get up early write it on votive paper and offer it to the gentle dawn breeeze *Is this correct She"?*

8. **Black Isis** and the **'Immaculate Conception'** and annunciation 'in a dream', that the child to be born from her was the offspring of a God.

Anahita [Persian] Great Goddess of the Waters, Ardvi Sura Anahita the Heavenly Spring from which all waters on the earth flow down; A Cleansing Day

Feast of the Immaculate Conception of the Blessed **Virgin Mary**.

Bodhi Day (Rohatsu) - Buddhism

The Great She Bear Shamaness - the Grandmother of the indigenous North American

9. **The Optalia**, the festival of Ops, the Roman Goddess of harvest.

The Virgin of Guadalupe [Mexican]- an old Aztec sky-goddess, who became the patron saint of all Mexico

The Unluckiest Day Of the Year – According to Grafton, the 16th century astrologer

9-16 Hannukah – Jewish

10. **Liberty** celebration in France. An actress is selected to personify the Goddess of Liberty. Being brought to Notre Dame, she is seated on the altar, and lights a large candle to signify that Liberty is the Light of the World.

12. 05:12 ○ FULL MOON

13. **The Sementivae**, the second festival of Tellus, the Roman earth Goddess.

14. 18:00 ♊ Geminid Meteor Shower

15. **The Second Festival Of Consus**, the Roman god of good council

17. **The Saturnalia**, First day of the seven-day festival of ♄ Saturn, the Roman god of agriculture. The most popular Roman festival. During this festival, business was suspended, the roles of master and slaves were reversed, moral restrictions were loosened, and gifts were exchanged. It was observed in memory of this Golden Age, at Saturn's temple on the Forum Romanum, below the Capitoline Hill.

18. 20:30 ○ Moon at Perigee: 370,260 km 06:30

19. 04:57 ◐ LAST QUARTER MOON

20. Festival for **Ammit/Al-Mawt** who was originally the ancestral spirit of the matriarchal culture in which the Feminine takes back what has been born of it. She was the underworld, the earth womb, as the perilous land of the dead through which the deceased must pass.

21. **Vesta** Capricorn was regarded as under the care of the goddess Vesta, and hence Vestae Sidus.

The Womb of Isis The adoration of the Mendesian Goat symbolised the Sun-God's resurrection in the House of the Goat (♑Capricorn) the Capricornian Goddess gives birth to the divine child of the next, year.

Amalthea [Greek] the nymph who fed Jupiter with goat's milk, one of whose horns broke off and was placed amongst the stars as Cornu Copiae, from which nectar and ambrosia were said to flow. Her principal star is Capella, the little goat. Therefore, Capricorn is the nurse of the youthful sun-god

Kore/Persephone The birth of the Divine Child, whether he bears the name of Horus, Osiris, Helios, Dionysus, or Aeon, was celebrated in the Koreion in Alexandria, the temple dedicated to Kore, on the day of the winter solstice.

Pryderi, [Celtic] son of Rhiannon, the virgin mother, is always born on the winter solstice.

♑CAPRICORN

Cardinal Sign of ▽ Earth.

22. 04:19 Solstice 14:19

23. 01:49 ♂ Mars 3°S of ○ Moon
03:00 Ursid Meteor Shower

0° ♑Capricorn ☼Sun enters ♑Capricorn.

Celtic **"No Name day."** Shortest day of the year in the northern Hemisphere. This day was considered a whole month in the Celtic calendar 13 months plus The No Name Day. This was the day when the ☼sun did not come above the horizon in the northern part of the British Isles. The mythos was that the God of light Lugus, descended into the underworld and rose again on Yuletide day. On this day, Yule logs, representing his dying body, were lit to light the way of the god back to the upper realms. On the 25th he is resurrected an immortal. This was symbolised and celebrate by the decorated evergreen tree.

The Larentalia (Larentinalia), festival of Acca Larentia the Roman Goddess who gave the early Romans their land. The earth-Goddess, also called Sabine and Dea Tacita, the silent Goddess, a Roman Goddess of dead. On this day, offerings were brought to her in a mundus, an opened groove. She was honoured on this day at an altar in the Velabrium.

24. **Last Day of the Saturnalia**
Modraniht, or 'Night of the Mothers', was so called as the day preceding 'Child's Day' or 'Yule Day' long before the Anglo-Saxons were exposed to Christianity, thus proving its real character. Inscriptions are known from Roman times in Germany, Holland, and Britain, honour of groups of female beings known generally as 'The Mothers'. Female deities of this kind seem to have been worshipped by both the Celts and the Germans, and they were evidently associated with fertility and with the protection of hearth and home.

25. Yule Eve Holiday. The Christian **Christmas Day,** At the end of the third century the Western Church adopted this pagan celebration (see below) day as the commemorative date of the birth of the Christos, and in time its decision was accepted also by the Eastern Church.

The Birthday Of Mithra, the Persian god of light and wisdom by his mother **Atargatis**.

Isis, the Virgo Caelestis, was believed to give birth to the Sun on the 25th of December.

Astarte festival celebrated in honour of the birth of the son of the Babylonian Queen of Heaven. **Myrrha** [Greek] The mother of Adonis, was changed into a tree, and then gave birth to her divine son. From this we get the custom of the putting of the Yule Log into the fire on. As **Zero-Ashta** (Seed of Woman,) or Ignigena – (Born of Fire) he has to enter the fire on 'Mother night' that he may be born the next day out of it.

The Girl of the Yule Log Sometimes the log would be dragged in with a girl enthroned on it. In Scandinavia the ash symbolised the wood of the world-tree, Yggdrasil, & would be sprinkled with corn.

The Star Fairy The Christmas Tree, with its bright baubles and the star on top is a miniature version of the World Tree of our pagan ancestors, with its roots deep in the earth, the sun, moon and stars hung on its spreading branches, and the Pole Star at its topmost point. Sometimes the Star is replaced by a Goddess, ruling over the World.

Dionysus/Bacchus was transformed into a tree to avoid murder by his jealous stepmother Hera. The Titans uprooted him and burnt him but he was resurrected. During the Saturnalia, a decorated pine tree was hung with little masks of Dionysus/Bacchus to commemorate this.

Nullog Day in Ancient Irish, meaning 'New Belly' 'being born anew'. They crawled through holes in the logs representing passing issuing through the womb to a new life.

26. 05:13 ● NEW MOON

05:18 ☼ Annular Solar Eclipse; SE Asia, partial NW Australia

Boxing Day – Day for giving gifts to the less fortunate and those that depend on you

Yule Tide Day - Day One Of the Twelve Days -Yule is related to Norse word 'Iul,' meaning 'Wheel' and 'Light', and Saxon word for 'Sun'. Ancient Egyptians at the Winter Solstice used a palm branch containing twelve leaves or shoots to symbolize the 'completion of the year'.

Sweetie Scone Day [Scotland] Scones and "Currant Loaf" were baked from the rich, sweet ingredients in the boxes given to the beneficiaries who could not afford the luxury of dried fruit and spices Neighbours would share ingredients and then share the sweets.

Zarathosht Diso Death of Prophet Zarathushtra – Zoroastrian

26 Dec - Jan 1 **Kwanzaa** – Interfaith.

27. 18:00 ♃ Jupiter Conjunction with ☼ Sun

Yule Eve Spiritual rebirth for old souls

Nut's Birthing Day After the twelfth month of each year and before the first day of the ensuing year, the Egyptians allowed five days to permit Nut to give birth to all her children.

Festival for The Horae, controllers of the wheel of time, who presided over all changes of time and watched over the works of men. They were goddesses of order in nature represented as delicate, joyous, lightly moving beings adorned with flowers and fruits.

29. 01:32 ♀ Venus 1°N of ◯ Moon: Occn.

The Egyptian remembrance of The Hours The Egyptians were the first to divide the day into 24 hours; there were twelve hours of the day and twelve to the night. Each was allocated a goddess standing in a boat, The 'Lady of the Boat' changed every hour.

30. On this day **Hathor gives birth to the sun Ra,** in the form of the Scarab beetle.

Isis birthday The Egyptian year consisted of twelve months of 30 days each making only 360 days: thus five intermediary days, called 'the thirteenth month', were added to make the year a complete 365. Isis, governed the fourth intercalary day, which was celebrated as her birthday.

31. New Year's Eve

Nephthys The fifth intercalary day was celebrated as the birthday of Nephthys,

Sekhmet Goddess of Time: If you get a vision of Sekhmet on this day will be fortunate.

Hestia/Vesta is the Genius of the home-fire, and it is traditional on this day to bless the house by making the Pentacle in the four corners of each room. Ivy is hung on the outer doors to protect the house against evil through the coming year.

Ancient Graeco-Egyptian New Years Eve Feast Set a luxurious table with exotic articles of food, and with goblets of new wine, for a fruitful New Year. The Egyptian year began at a different time from ours, but this is as near as possible the way in which Hogmanay is still observed on the last day of the last month of the year in Scotland.

Hogmanay is New Year's Night preceding the Hagmena, or Holy Month on which a table is spread, with buns and other dainties, oatcakes, cheese and strong drink is essential. For the Irish anything which happened on New Year's Eve and Day might divinity of the future, and the nearer to the midnight hour when the year actually began, the more significant.

Entering The Age of Cailleach Bheara corresponds to the maturity of humanity. This is an era of reawakened psychic and artistic sensitivity, of renewed magical powers and of growing religious knowledge.

Join us on line for times and sidereal astrological potential for each day for your magickal workings

Pete & Shelene's Fairy Tale Handfasting Sanctuary Cove Gold Coast

Magick Magazine No. 9

HELP PAGANISM TO BECOME A RECOGNISED DENOMINATION IN AUSTRALIA

I am a "Religious" Pagan marriage celebrant.
I am *the "last" legal religious Pagan celebrant"* in Australia.

PLEASE SIGN OUR PETITION HERE:
https://www.change.org/p/attorney-general-s-department-allow-paganism-to-become-a-recognised-denomination-in-australia

Our government has deemed all celebrants, civil, unless they are from a registered religion, which I am. However, they will not allow any other celebrants to become "religious Pagan" unless Paganism becomes a registered denomination. Sadly, even though there are many registered Pagan churches and groups ready to band together to become a denomination, the Attorney General's Department is not allowing our application for an umbrella Pagan religious denomination to go through. Thirty-six Pagan religious organisations have banded together to do this. Yet, the Australian Attorney-General's Department's reason for the denial is because "They" don't consider Paganism to be an organised religion.

So, an arbitrary decision has been made, a judgment call, by someone with opposing religious views, hidden behind a desk somewhere, to limit your religious freedom. This decision affects every Australian and Pagan, all around the world. You have to tell them that is not acceptable. Say "NO" loudly and clearly. Otherwise, in the near future we may not be able to hold beautiful ceremonies like this, legally, any more   - https://youtu.be/GsQALE_Te1I   and we will have **moved back one step closer to the dark ages** and a **return to the witch hunts.**

STAND UP & SAY "**NO**" TO THAT!!!!

It would be wonderful if we all could show support for religious freedom, of a group that has no dogma, is empowering, honours the individual, follows a nature based belief system, that is highly ethical, has no extremist history and that hurts no one. In fact, during the recent 'Royal Commission into Victimisation by Religious Organisations' there were "zero" complaints lodged against any Pagan group or organisation. However, what we really do, is hold beautiful and meaningful ceremonies like the handfasting in this Youtube clip.

Please show your support for what Australia could loose if Pagan Religious celebrants become extinct with my demise. **Please demand that your religious freedoms be upheld by signing this petition.**

Thank You & Every Bright Blessing to you,
Reverend. Dr S. D'Montford (D.D. HPs)

http://www.shedmontford.com/magickal-weddings.html

THEDA BARA

Theda Bara (July 29, 1885 - April 7, 1955) was an American silent film and stage actress. She was the original goth model and horror movie anti-heroine. Bara was one of the most popular actresses of the silent era, and one of cinema's earliest sex symbols. Her riské femme fatale roles earned her the nickname *The Vamp* (short for "vampire") later fuelling the rising popularity in "vamp" roles that encapsulated, partial nudity, exoticism and sexual domination. Her screen name made an anagram "Death Arab" and fuelled her dark mystique, though people described her as *"...very normal in every day life"*. Bara made more than 40 films between 1914 and 1926, but most were lost in the 1937 Fox vault fire. After her marriage to Charles Brabin in 1921, she made two more feature films and then retired from acting in 1926, having never appeared in a sound film. Several magickal orders claim her as a member.

BOOKS BY SHÉ D'MONTFORD

DEMONOLOGY — $20
The belief in demons is not universal. Follow the history of the creation of demons to discover what they really are

IBOGAINE — $20
An ancient cure for addiction in one treatment without withdrawals

GOETIA — $20
A modern translation of this text on how to work with the Goeting beings without the overlay of Christian culture demonisation

SCRYING: THE ART OF SEEING THE FUTURE WITH OMENS & DIVINATION — $25
Tea Leaf Reading, Runes, Oghams, Gematria, Dreams, Clouds, Fire, Chinese Ink and more

SEVEN PSYCHIC SECRETS — $25
BEST SELLER – Seeing Auras, Moving & Feeling Energy, Psychometry, Remote Viewing, Working With Spirit, Healing & Remote healing

QUICK SPELLS — $10
For the seven most wished for things

THE INNER GODDESS WORKOUT — $29
40 Goddesses & how to work with them - Illustrations by Wanda Shipton

THE CANCER ANSWER — $10
Legitimate, Approved effective cure, that is that has been available since 1950 but that the medical industry will not tell you about. WHY?

WHO'S AFRAID OF THE BIG BAD WITCH? — $29
Exploding the most common Lies about the Craft of the Wise

WOMEN WHO MARRY ANGELS: — $25
Collected Works of Ida Craddock

SPIRIT SHOTS — $29
200 photos of ghosts and spirits. What is death & how to work with the spirit realm.

PENDULUM DOWSING: — $10
Discover the Secrets of Dowsing

IMPROVE PHYSICAL AND SPIRITUAL VISION — $10
Physical and spiritual exercises to improve your vision

THE MAGIC STORY — $10
The Secret of Success - Written in 1700s, Rewritten in 1901. Reprinted today, More relevant than ever

MAGICK 8: FOR THOSE WHO BELIEVE — $12.95
Back Issue

AVAILABLE FROM ALL GOOD BOOK STORES - Distributed through Ingram Spark

A WILD DOLPHIN QUEST

Dolphins, in myth are often **rescuers of humans, bring them back to the surface. Resurface and Breath** is the centre of dolphin magick. **Re-centre & Re-Surface** from whatever is drowning you and **find your joy again.** Dolphins do indeed purposely rescue people in danger. Dolphins have been safeguarding and teaching humans for millennia. The 'White Dolphin Dreaming' in Australia where the dolphins herd the fish into the nets for the fishermen. In ancient Greece, Poseidon sent a dolphin to save his son from a shipwreck. For the ancient Romans, dolphins were in charge of bringing the souls of the dead to the 'Islands of the Blessed' The wise have always associated dolphins with the mystical processes of life, death, and resurrection. It was terrible luck to harm a dolphin but great luck to see one. You were blessed by the gods if you have a personal encounter or become surrounded by a playful pod .
Let me share this blessing of the gods with you.

A once in a life time trip to change your life and the way that you look at your place in the world in relation to our animal brothers and sisters.

Dolphin wisdom begins with learning to live immersed in joy. Plunge freely into these safe crystalline waters. These are the world's clearest, bluest waters, where you will meet and have fun, hanging out with the ocean's smartest, most sociable animals.

"Wildquest was truly spectacular. I had the best week of my life..."

Meeting dolphins in the wild, on their own terms, is magical. An instant plug-in to being in the 'here and now'. A re-connection with your own joy.

It's our joy to make it so, so easy for you. We take care of every detail. WildQuest with Shé D'Montford is a gathering of like minded heroic souls that quickly becomes a 'human pod'. Where you can find a place to belong.

"...I am a 48 yr old single woman. I love life. I enjoy life. But I have always wanted to swim with wild dolphins. When you see the website and videos, it's like 'Yeh that would be nice but bet it's not real." Well it is!!! ITS REAL..."

'Embark upon a spiritual journey discovering your animal totems and animal communication within a relaxing mix of sailing open seas, dolphin swims, healthy delicious food (organic when possible) a laid-back Retreat Centre for chilling out and enjoying the program of the week. Designed to re-connect you with your own body, so you can connect with the dolphins when they come to greet you.

"...Very real. From the moment we went out in the boat we saw wild dolphins. They swim right up to the boat, you get in the water and they come right up to you. They check you out, look at you, swim around you, alongside you, with you. Its amazing..."

WildQuest with Shé D'Montford is an uplifting, gentle adventure where you will bond with new friends, dolphin and human. This WildQuest retreat with Shé D'Montford includes **FOUR**(4) Animal Communication, Animal Totems and Psychic Development workshops. Additionally, each person will receive a personal private session/healing/reading with Shé D'Montford. These amazing extras are valued at over $1000.

Happy, Healing & Harmonious.

"...I stayed there Sept 2013. ...the experience was life changing for me ... and for everyone...."

This is a sacred journey & a retreat with Shé D'Montford Kind, knowledgeable, full of heart and very friendly. Shé has the ability to change people. On this trip Shé will reconnect you with the oceans, the source of life. Shé was the bikini girl on the Australian TV series "Flipper." Most of us grew up dreaming of having a personal connection with dolphins like they had on that show. Well, now you can. Every day for weeks at a time, Shé was in the water with the dolphins at Sea World. Additionally, Shé has worked as a professional animal psychic with the Dr. Fabian Fay, the legendary vet from Sea World Australia. Shé got to know dolphins very well. Let Shé show you how you can share the dolphin's secret wisdom. Shé's one goal on this trip is to create a sacred journey into the dolphins world, for you to meet the mystery of the ocean and most importantly, the sacred within you.

".... they welcome you into their world, into their pod... they will come to you and swim around you. At one time, had 11 dolphins swimming all around me. It was like the best dream I ever had, BUT IT WAS REAL !..."

Yoga and Meditation are a main part of the week, (but optional if you'd rather do your own thing). Designed to relax you ready to meet the dolphins from a rested, stilled space. The easier you breathe on land and in the water, the easier it is to connect with the dolphins. Yoga is also a great way to stretch, open up, tone and strengthen the body. Your body, your beautiful vehicle on this planet, will appreciate it.

"...I had to remember to breath, it was so breathtaking! There were babies too!... "

You will see transformation happen. This is far more than a memorable holiday, more than a vacation from your usual self. This experience is powerful, expansive and heartfelt. Shé D'Montoford's workshops included in the programme will allow you to learn something new and let go of the old. There'll be much laughter, maybe tears, great new friendships and moments you'll never forget. **This wilderness experience**, is designed to re-connect you with yourself, with others, the dolphins, and all living beings in a loving supportive environment!

"...I didn't want to ever leave. It is the only time I have felt i could be the real me....."

Meeting the dolphins is magical. They're just being what they really are. By example they show you how to be the same. In their presence you will find yourself letting go and blissing out. They help us plug back into our hearts. Meeting, being to being. No ego, no boundaries, pure presence. Connection. A resonance of oneness many seek through prolonged spiritual practice.

"...The people who come on this trip are different, in the best way, so life aware... after one day we were like our own pod. I have made friendships that will last through my life..."

What a delightful combination. Nurturing exercise, mindfulness, wholesome healthy food, lazy days cruising out into open, warm, aquamarine seas to find the dolphins, chilling out on a boat-full of like-minded people, with loving support from all crew.

"....The people, food, accommodation, boat, meditations, healings were all fantastic. I can't fault one thing...... The accommodation was great. Air con, comfy bed, fridge, ensuite. Food was amazing, all healthy and tasted great....

This WildQuest with Shé D'Montford will leave you rejuvenated. Full again, with the joys of life and a renewed sense of connection.

*...I miss the dolphins, the people and the place so much already. I took a go-pro camera, so have loads of videos of the dolphins underwater, so so amazing !!!! I will definitely keep going back again and again. (I'm happy to answer any questions, but beware I will talk for ages hehe....) Thank you Wildquest you are **the highlight of my life** xx - Barbi*

This retreat in September 2020 on Bimini Is in the Bahamas, is with the rare spotted dolphins. It is strictly limited to only 20 people - We would love to have you join us on this magical adventure, so hurry to secure your once in a life time opportunity. Early bird discounts are available until Oct 20th 2019.

BOOK YOUR WILDQUEST DOLPHIN RETREAT WITH SHÉ D'MONTFORD NOW

0488 495 185

Email Questions To Us

Magick Magazine No. 9

READERS FUNNY PHOTOS

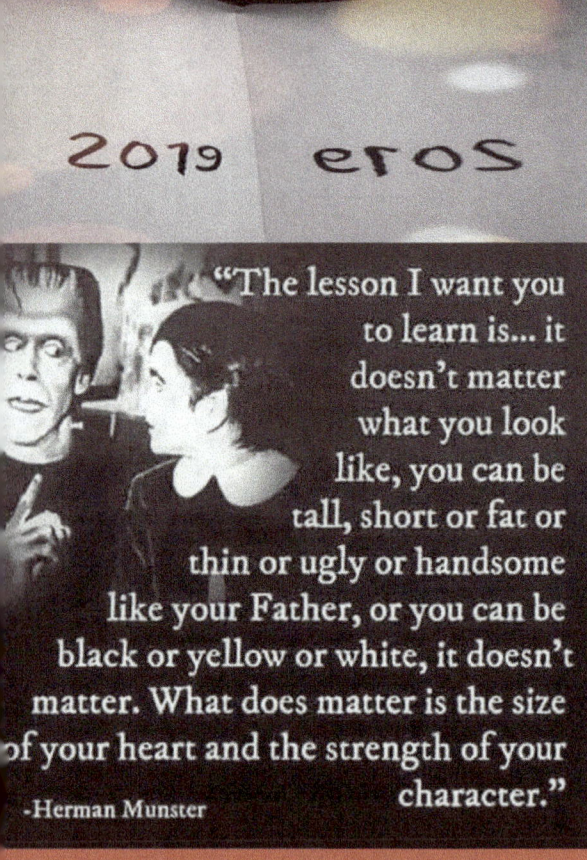

Submitted by Chin Chillax who says: "The only acceptable way to use love potion!"

MAGICK PHOTO WINNER

Miriam Watt - "I stopped by St James Park the other day (on totally above board definitely not clandestine business) and while watching the ducks a pair of celestial visitors sat down!"

MAGICKAL CLASSIFIDES

MYSTICAL REALMS WITCHCRAFT
Australia

A place where magical energies come together, entwining the uniqueness of each individual's own spiritual path to proudly celebrate who we are. You will fit in at Mystic Realms Witchcraft

- Gatherings • Workshops • Esbat
- Sabbats • Unique and needful things for the craft of the wise

Go to www.mysticalrealmswitchcraft.com for upcoming events and other useful stuff.
Remember to like us on Facebook

REMEMBER
Go to our facebook page & send us a message about your free/non-profit magickal events so that we can list it here & tell everyone in the community !
https://www.facebook.com/MagickMagazine/

Astrovisuals
Supplying Astronomical Visual Materials including Calendars, Apps, Star & Moon maps & novelties. Manufactured in Australia.
mail@astrovisuals.com.au
https://www.astrovisuals.com/
0431 193 396

TAKE A SELFIE
reading Magick Magazine. Make the photo memorable or in an amazing location. Then send it to us for a chance to win great prizes & you might even see yourself in the pages of Magick too!

UP COMING EVENTS
FAIRYUTOPIA Guinness World Record: Sat 24 Aug 2019

CHECK OUR WEBSITE FOR UPDATES
WWW.MYSTICEVENTS.COM.AU
touch.newage@icloud.com

0459 511 444

THE AWAKENING
BRISBANE TIVOLI THEATRE
ANNUAL IMBOLC WITCHES MASQUERADE BALL
3RD OF AUGUST 2019
EARLY BIRD TICKETS ON SALE NOW
WWW.MYSTICALREALMSWITCHCRAFT.COM

NEXT EVENT 2019 THE AWAKENING Imbolc Brisbane Witches Masquerade Ball
Come join us at the Annual Brisbane Witches Masquerade Ball August 3rd 2019, Hosted by Mystic Realms

REMEMBER
CHECK OUR PAGES
for more magickal competitions and giveaways from our advertisers, events and other cool stuff
www.magick.org.au
Facebook
https://www.facebook.com/MagickMagazine/
Group
https://www.facebook.com/groups/magickmagazine/

GOLD COAST WITCHES' BREW
A friendly, informal coffee morning for those interested in Witchcraft, Wicca, Druidry or any other form of Paganism and/or Earth Based Spirituality.
ALL WELCOME!
WHEN: Last Monday of each month from 10.30am to approx 12.30pm
WHERE: Cafe Campanile, Robina Town Centre, Gold Coast, Queensland.
Want more details?
Phone: 0402066330 or
Email: morganna13@hotmail.com

Woman's Spiritual Wiccan Coven of Gold Coast
Live life magically and spiritually attuned with nature. Fortnightly to Monthly Meet Ups. To find out more go to
www.meetup.com/WiccanCoven

REMEMBER: Go to our facebook page & send us a message about your free/non-profit magickal events so that we can list it here & tell everyone in the community !

Professional Psychic Reading Service is located in Gold Coast, Australia. We helped change the lives of hundreds of satisfied customers from around the world through psychic readings.
www.barbspsychicreadings.com

Barb's Psychic Readings
0450 593 196

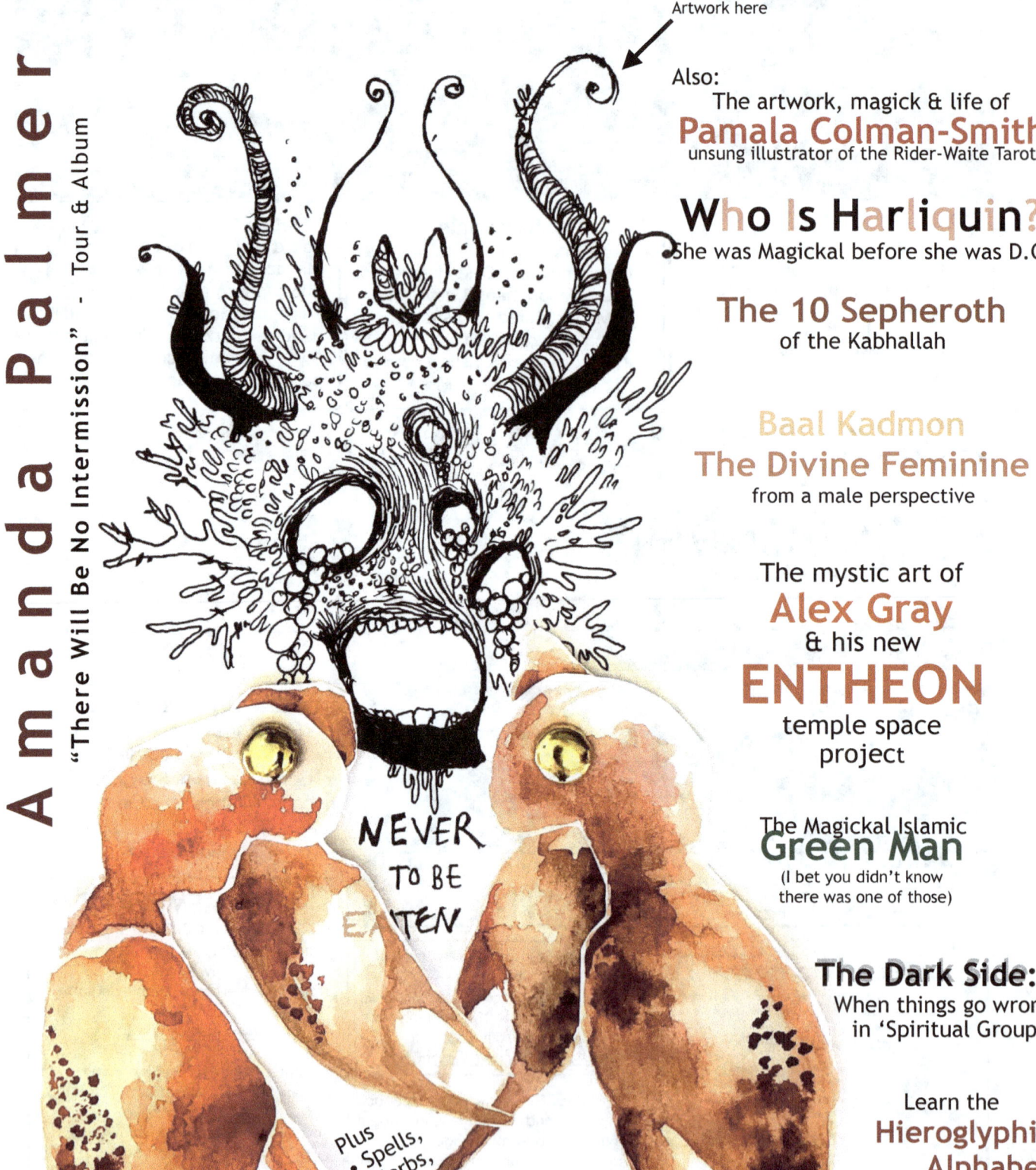

Our Next Magick Magazine: We will be TEN

It is our BIG tenth issue

Amanda Palmer — "There Will Be No Intermission" - Tour & Album

Plus
- Spells,
- Herbs,
- Events
- Reviews,
- The Weekly Seer
- Erotic Pagan Fiction
- The Witches' Almanac
- & much, much, more!

And a few surprises too!!!

We will feature rising Pagan/Magickal Monster & 3D artist
Joey Potter

Artwork here

Also:
The artwork, magick & life of
Pamala Colman-Smith
unsung illustrator of the Rider-Waite Tarot

Who Is Harliquin?
She was Magickal before she was D.C.

The 10 Sepheroth
of the Kabhallah

Baal Kadmon
The Divine Feminine
from a male perspective

The mystic art of
Alex Gray
& his new
ENTHEON
temple space project

The Magickal Islamic
Green Man
(I bet you didn't know there was one of those)

The Dark Side:
When things go wrong in 'Spiritual Groups'

Learn the
Hieroglyphic Alphabet

Order Now:
www.magick.org.au

78

MAGICK MAGAZINE
WILL COMMENCE ITS OWN
ONLINE COURSE IN MAGICK
2019

EVERYONE CAN PERFORM MAGICK. To a lesser extent we do it every day. Our WILL shapes our world. We make sure that we get the things we like & influence people to see things our way. But we can learn to do so much more. You can learn to do Magick far more effectively. We can get results in a scientifically repeatable way.

SHÉ D'MONTFORD WILL SHOW YOU HOW.

Learn esoteric skills from **AURA SEEING** to **THE ZIGI**. Learn magickal methods from **INDIGENOUS MAGICK** of the Australia Aborigines through to the **HIGH MAGICK** of the elite ceremonial magickians. From **BASIC CANDLE** & **SIGAL MAGICK** through to **TIME TRAVEL & TRANSCENDENCE**.

THESE ARE TESTED METHODS THAT WORK!

Shé has a deep, extensive curriculum that she has taught around the world since 1990. Shé teaches magick without the nonsense. Magick, when you do it right, is not that hard. Learning the right way from a good teacher is the necessary thing. View the curriculum online www.shedmontford.com/curriculum.html Now, Shé D'Montford's classes are moving into the digital age to make all the Magick available to you in a practical & easy to learn package. These classes will be live & pre-recorded, online courses, with the ability to interact directly with Shé D'Montford & ask her questions.

Shé D'Montford has been traveling around the world to make herself available to teach empowering magick to eager students in person. Now, with the aid of digital technology, Shé can be available to all sincere seekers, anywhere in the world, all the time, Packages will bundle together units that are usually about $95 each, for the low price of only $25 per month. YOU can save thousands & YOU can have personal tuition no matter where in the world YOU live, whenever it is convenient for YOU to learn.

Sign up for to our exclusive subscribers group, for as little as $25 per month & enjoy having full access to all that you can possibly learn or you can purchase specific packages. There is a recommended order to the lessons to help you progress. Join up for your no risk beginners course today. There is a 30-day money back guarantee if you are not happy & you can unsubscribe at any time.

GO TO   www.magick.org.au   & BEGIN A MAGICKAL LIFE TODAY

BONUS:
Every subscriber receives Magick Magazine for free for the duration of their subscription to their magickal tuition.

www.ingramcontent.com/pod-product-compliance
Lightning Source LLC
Chambersburg PA
CBHW080900010526
44118CB00015B/2217